I0540569

José Silva's
EVERYDAY
ESP
Master Course

José Silva's

EVERYDAY

ESP

Master Course

Unlock Your Natural God-Given Intuition

Complete Step-by-Step Guide

José Silva and Ed Bernd Jr.

No part of this book may be reproduced or transmitted in any form, by any means, (electronic, photocopying, recording, or otherwise) without the prior written permission of the author. No liability is assumed with respect to the use of the information contained within. Although every precaution has been taken, the author and publisher assume no liability for errors or omissions. Neither is any liability assumed for damages resulting from the use of the information contained herein.

JOSÉ SILVA'S EVERYDAY ESP MASTER COURSE. Copyright © 2026 by Silva Method UltraMind LLC

The Silva Method is the registered trademark of Silva International Inc.

For more genuine Jose Silva books and products please visit SilvaMethodUltraMind.com

Edited by David Aretha

Front Cover design by David Rheinhardt of Pyrographx
Interior design by Meghan Day Healey of Story Horse, LLC

Library of Congress Cataloging-in-Publication Data is available upon request

ISBN: 978-1-965725-28-3 (Paperback)
ISBN: 978-1-965725-29-0 (Paperback Large Print Edition)

ISBN: 978-1-7225-0753-4 (Hardcover)
ISBN: 978-1-7225-2883-6 (epub)
ISBN: 978-1-7225-5451-4 (Audio book)

10 9 8 7 6 5 4 3 2 1

CONTENTS

Part 3 Universal ESP Training

Part 4 Silva Success Stories

Part 5 Advanced Techniques for Psychics

Appendix

INTRODUCTION
by José Silva Jr.

Welcome and congratulations on taking the first steps into the 2nd Phase of Human Evolution on the Planet.

This Master Course guides you to develop and actually use your psychic ability. This allows you to expand your consciousness throughout the universe and beyond.

We will examine psychic research from around the globe, from South Texas to the Soviet Union, conducted by starry-eyed optimists, deadly Cold War spies, and others.

It exposes the truth about your own ESP that you might not realize you already have and how you can benefit from it right now.

How to Use This Book

The book is divided into five parts. It is like having five books in one so you can utilize them in the way that suits you best.

For some people this will be a series of brief how-to books.

Others think of it as a comprehensive textbook.

It is also a reference manual, a training manual, a historical reference work.

It all depends on what you need at this moment in time.

Some readers are new to our work and need to learn the basics.

Readers who have already taken our training can choose the sections and chapters they need.

To begin your ESP training immediately, go to Chapter 12 and learn how to find the alpha brainwave level, then continue with the chapters in order through Chapter 21.

It is okay to read other chapters as long as you make sure to do the lessons in Chapters 12 through 21 in order the first time, because each one builds on the previous lessons.

Here is what you will learn in each of the 5 Parts:

Psychic Ability Simplified

In Part 1 of this book you will meet some naturally developed psychics, and you will learn several alternative ways you can use to access some of your latent psychic ability.

We will pull back the curtain and reveal how various ESP techniques and devices actually work. Some have physical explanations while others require us to go beyond physics to understand them.

Part 2 reveals the mindset that has made so many Silva students so successful. Students of knock-off courses of my father's work often fail to get comparable results.

Part 3 contains the complete Silva ESP training used by millions of people worldwide since the 1960s to develop their natural God-given psychic ability.

There are three simple steps:

1. Learn to enter the alpha brainwave level and activate your mind by using visualization and imagination.
2. While at the alpha level do some mental projection exercises to correlate what you detect mentally with what you experience with your physical senses.

3. After you have established these mental points of reference, we explain how to develop your expertise with them by working on real problem cases.

We provide clear explanations every step of the way so you can begin right now and change your life for the better.

Part 4 has a collection of success stories and examples of people using their Silva ESP training in all areas of life. These will help you discover the possibilities of what you can achieve.

Part 5 provides several advanced strategies and techniques to help you use your ESP more efficiently in all areas of your life.

Let Me Ask You a Simple Question:

Isn't it time you learned how to use your mind the way that ultra-successful people do?

My father always believed that God doesn't play favorites when it comes to having the tools you need to live a productive, prosperous, and meaningful life.

That was his belief when my ten-year-old sister Isabel started "guessing his mind" in 1953.

He had been using hypnosis to help her remember her school lessons. Then one day she started answering before he told her what the questions was.

He had been skeptical when he read that some people have psychic ability, and now it appeared he had trained Isabel to be a psychic.

He wrote to the leading ESP researcher at the time, Dr. J. B. Rhine at Duke University, the man who coined the term ESP. Dr. Rhine assured him that Isabel had always been psychic; he just hadn't noticed it before.

Neither man ever backed down, and my father said that when they met in person a decade later, they almost came to blows.

In a way, both men were right:

Nobody can give you something you already have.

We all have psychic ability.

Why You Need to Develop Your Intuition and Learn to Use It Reliably

You know your mind can impress information on your brain neurons and then retrieve this information when you need it. That's called "memory."

You can also use your mind to detect information that has been impressed on other people's brain neurons. That is called ESP.

You can do more than detect information from other people's brains: You can find out how they used that information, how they applied it, and what their results were.

In other words, you can learn about other people's experiences, and you can use their experiences as if they were your own.

You can also learn what their hopes and dreams are and what they want in life. Silva UltraMind ESP Systems graduates know that helping other people get what they want will usually help you get what you want.

Imagine the Possibilities

Silva graduates report that ESP has helped them:

- Get a job, a raise, a promotion; find meaningful work
- Choose the right career with meaningful work and the correct work/life balance
- Make the right move at the right time to avoid danger and seize opportunities
- Understand what's causing their child's bad behavior and the most beneficial way to correct it
- To know what's bothering their children so they can guide them and help them mature into confident, kind, and successful adults
- Pick the perfect partner for friendship, business, romance, family
- Choose the best doctor and the ideal lifestyle to help them live a long, healthy, productive life
- Improve relationships by understanding themself and others on a deeper level so they know the right things to say and do to satisfy the other person
- Influence people's thoughts; guide them to the decision that is best for everybody concerned
- Experience spiritual growth and understanding
- Enhance creativity
- Make better decisions
- Convert challenges into opportunities and successes
- Project into challenges to discover fresh perspectives and find innovative solutions
- Quickly identify and dismiss liars, cheaters, and scammers

- Find missing persons
- Solve crimes
- Develop wisdom, good judgment, and good decision-making ability, and be right more often than wrong

Live a meaningful life by improving living conditions on the planet so that when we move on we shall have left behind a better world for those who follow

Dependable Intuition Is Like Money in the Bank

It is no secret that geniuses use more of their minds and use them in a special manner.

Imagine how valuable it would be if you knew how to access that psychic information whenever you need it to help you make the right decision, to influence your children or someone else.

That's the ability that the most successful people have and the average person is missing:

The ultra-successful have expanded their consciousness into two dimensions.

The good news is that all you need is somebody to help you access the dormant area of your brain where it is stored, and then help you learn how to use it. That is what this ESP Master Course will do for you with just a few weeks of practice.

ESP is revolutionizing many fields and changing millions of people's lives for the better, and you are invited to join them in unlocking superpowers you probably hadn't realized you have.

What Does the Future Hold?

In today's competitive marketplace, you need every advantage you can get.

Wouldn't you love to know what to expect during the coming months and years?

Super-successful people know.

How do they know?

They use their natural God-given ESP.

My father put it this way:

"The difference between genius mentality and lay mentality is that geniuses use more of their mind and use it in a special manner."

In this Master Course you will learn to do what only a fortunate few have been able to do and use your intuition to detect information not available to the average person to help you make better decisions and solve more problems.

If You Can Dream It You Can Do It

Imagine a world where we all have everything we need without taking from anyone else, without hurting anybody. Imagine a world where people know how to use their mind to understand themselves and others better and find solutions that are best for everybody concerned.

It would truly be a paradise on Earth.

You can help make that vision a reality by learning how to actually use the hidden talents you already have.

Leaders in Mind Development and ESP Since 1944

My father, personally and through the thousands of Silva instructors he has trained, has helped millions of people learn to change their lives for the better. This course will guide you step-by-step to learn his techniques and systems in the privacy and convenience of your own home.

Now, after more than 80 years in this field, using written information and recordings that my father left with us, we can offer you a streamlined and enhanced version of the world-famous ESP training he developed and tested from 1944 to 1966.

It has been streamlined by eliminating features he included to help skeptics accept the new ideas.

It has been enhanced with a couple of additional ESP techniques that will boost your belief in your ability to use advanced ESP even before you complete the training.

And his ultimate ESP technique enables you to communicate directly with higher intelligence on the "other side" to obtain guidance and help when you need it to solve problems and implement solutions that will improve living conditions on the planet.

Special Information for Parents

In addition to all of that, in Chapter 10 he reveals a simple procedure he discovered in his research that helps parents help their children grow up with complete psychic ability.

That was his final gift to humanity shortly before his passing, and this Master Course contains what you need to ensure that your children will be geniuses.

Meet Your Instructors

This book is a collaborative effort of my father, through his writings, lectures, recordings, and private conversations, along with me and longtime editor and collaborator Ed Bernd Jr.

Material written or recorded by my father is clearly identified. Some of it may be edited for clarity, brevity, and grammar just as we did when he was alive.

Ed has been working with us here in Laredo, Texas, since 1981. He coauthored several books with my father, and he coauthored our newest book with me: *José Silva's Everyday ESP*. He has also developed several seminars and home-study courses under my father's guidance and direction.

Start Today

If you are ready to learn to unleash the untapped power of your mind to make a real difference in your relationships, your work, your family, your community, your world, and in all of the things that matter the most to you, then follow the instructions in this book and take the first steps in a journey to a whole new world, a subjective world—the world of the mind—where everything is possible.

Thank you, and as my father used to say, we look forward to working for you and with you.

Part 1
7 Kinds of ESP

CHAPTER 1

What Are Naturally Developed Psychics?

by José Silva

The original definition of ESP meant "extra sensory perception," but scientific research has proven that definition to be inaccurate.

ESP is not an "extra" sense. It is a prior sense, something everyone has but not everyone develops and uses consciously.

It is the master sensing faculty of human intelligence. It is not limited by time and space like your physical senses.

So we have retained the familiar initials—ESP—and changed the meaning to Effective Sensory Projection.

Why Aren't We All Natural Psychics?

Even though we are all born with natural psychic ability, only 10 percent of people continue to use and develop that ability as they grow up. Ninety percent of humans develop their physical senses but not their mental sensing faculties.

Those 90 percent might still have flashes of insight. You might have had moments when your intuition was working for you even though you had no training at all to develop this faculty.

During alpha dream time, some people have "precognitive" dreams—they dream of something, and then it happens shortly afterward.

How Natural Clairvoyants Function

Natural clairvoyants don't know how they did it, or what happened in their lives to be able to concentrate in that special manner that they developed the use of the right brain hemisphere.

Natural clairvoyants can be 100 percent. Natural ones can't teach it to anyone because they don't know how they got it. Each of them is different from the other. Sometimes they turn on; sometimes they don't. They have some trigger for their clairvoyance, like being in a rocking chair or hearing bells. Once at their clairvoyant level, they sometimes might not be able to come out.

"Naturals" can learn our system and improve their ability.

How Psychic Ability Works

You have two sets of senses for detecting information about people, places, things, and events.

Information you detect with your objective—physical—senses is impressed on the left brain hemisphere, and a copy is transferred to the right brain hemisphere.

Information you detect with your subjective—psychic—senses is impressed on your right brain hemisphere. But for most people nothing is transferred to their left hemisphere.

Therefore, most people—90 percent—only have conscious access to information they detected with their physical senses.

Their right brain hemisphere has twice as much information as the left, but they don't know how to access it or retrieve it.

The intuitive faculty is a faculty of the right brain hemisphere. The left brain hemisphere is logical. It has to do with mathematics and logic and so on. The right one has the so-called deductive faculty of mind, they call it.

The best you can say is that a natural clairvoyant as well as a trained clairvoyant is only 80 percent accurate in what they come up with, information-wise. Now, when we say 80 percent accurate done by the naturals as well as trained, we find something here:

We need to be able to eliminate the 20 percent error.

Cannot Choose When to Use Their ESP

In testing these people, we cannot eliminate or reduce the 20 percent error factor in the natural ones because the natural clairvoyants did not know they were clairvoyants to begin with.

They did not know how they became clairvoyant.

If they don't know how they became clairvoyant, they cannot teach it to anybody else or control it.

Sometimes they don't want to be clairvoyant.

Sometimes they do want to be clairvoyant but cannot turn it on.

Trained clairvoyants can control it.

Seeing that we do not have common denominators within the natural clairvoyants, we cannot test them to eliminate the error.

We can test the trained clairvoyants because they were all trained by the same method. They know exactly what they went through to become clairvoyant, so now they can teach it to others.

Now, we have common denominators. We can get clairvoyants together and correlate their information.

Though we cannot correlate the information of natural clairvoyants, we can correlate the information of trained clairvoyants and eliminate or reduce the percentage of error.

Examples of Some Natural Clairvoyants
by Ed Bernd Jr.

In 1956 Jeanne Dixon, a well-known psychic, wrote an article for a national magazine predicting that the United States' 1960 presidential election would be won by a Democrat who would be assassinated while in office.

In 1963 she became more concerned and tried to warn President John F. Kennedy several time. On the morning of November 22, 1963, she told friends that this was the day it would happen. But since she didn't know any specifics of who or how the attack might take place, there was nothing the security professionals could do.

Shortly after noon President John F. Kennedy was shot and killed while riding in a motorcade in Dallas, Texas.

A couple of generations later, in 2001, a natural psychic in California named Elena Wagner Rynkevic learned the value of knowing how to send information psychically as well as receiving psychic messages.

She wanted to improve her psychic ability in order to increase her sales, so she bought a copy of The Silva UltraMind ESP System audio workshop.

Her sales tripled.

Pleased with that, she went to her level one evening and sent out a thought: "Please show me something of importance."

She got an image of a city skyline she was very familiar with: New York City. But something was missing—the World Trade Center wasn't there. She went to level again the next night and asked for clarification, but the images she got frustrated her: the "Twin Towers" were gone. That was September 10, 2001.

The attack on the World Trade Center was the next day, destroying the Twin Towers and killing nearly 3,000 people.

Limitations That Natural Psychics Often Face

Both Jeane Dixon and Elena Rynkevic had visions of the attacks against the United States. Neither at the time knew how to get to their psychic level and take action to prevent the attack. There are a couple of obvious reasons:

They didn't have a specific system to get to the level where they could apply preventive measures.

They didn't have training or experience taking action to solve the problems they detected.

Elena Rynkevic took immediate steps to correct that deficiency: She called us and made arrangements to come to Laredo and learn our complete UltraMind ESP System immediately.

"When I told Ed Bernd Jr. my story, he explained to me that we can change the future," she recalled. "He said that prophetic visions are warnings so we can make changes, or if we cannot change it, to prepare ourselves to deal with it."

That gave Elena a new tool that Jeanne Dixon and most other naturally developed psychics do not have: A reliable way to change the future.

Knowing the Future

How do we get information about something that hasn't happened yet?

Because we can detect the plans that people are making. José Silva explained it this way:

The past is composed of materialized thoughts.

The present is the process of materializing thought.

The future is composed of conceived thoughts that have not yet been materialized.

Conceived thoughts are impressed on the brain neurons of the person who conceives them. When they act on those thoughts, the results are also impressed on their brain neurons, so they can learn what works for them and what doesn't.

Now, let's look at a case where a psychic's knowledge of what was coming allowed her to save a patient's life.

Projecting Mentally into a Patient's Head
Saved His Life

José Silva's daughter Isabel, a nurse anesthetist, gave us a wonderful example at Instructor training one year.

She had recently started work at a new hospital and doctors hadn't gotten to know about her special abilities yet. She was in the emergency room when a patient was brought in with a serious head injury. Here is what happened:

The surgeon relied on what he could see when he looked at the patient and at the equipment that was scanning the patient's brain. He didn't see any indication of bleeding in the brain.

Meanwhile, Isabel projected her mental senses—her mind—into the patient's head and realized that profuse bleeding was about to begin. So she told the doctor they needed to prep the operating room immediately.

The doctor told her she was wrong and ignored her.

Isabel went into the operating room anyway and told them to get ready; they would have a patient coming in shortly.

Then she went back into the ER and again urged the surgeon to move the patient into the OR immediately.

"There's no bleeding," he snapped back at her. "Look at the monitor. There's no . . . *Oh my God, he's bleeding! Get him into the OR now!*"

Everything was already set up in the operating room, and that probably saved the patient's life thanks to Isabel's dedication to solving problems whenever she had the opportunity.

The surgeon was one of the 90 percent of people who only have access to what they can see, hear, smell, and feel with their physical senses and physical instruments.

Isabel had access to all of that *plus* what she could detect with her subjective—psychic—senses.

What Life Is Like for a Lucky Man

It applies to all fields: Business people who rely only on what they can see and hear and touch and taste and smell to make management decisions are severely limited compared to those who use their psychic senses effectively.

Physical senses can be blocked, as happened with the surgeon. Nothing can block your mind. But you have to use it. That's what you will learn to do in Part 3.

One of the people José Silva studied described himself as "a lucky man."

"I got to meet a man," Silva recalled, "who said, 'You know, Mr. Silva, no matter what I do, I end up with more money. I mean, people come out of the woodwork just to give me money. Money, money, money, money. I don't know what's going on, but everything I do, I end up with more money.' He was very wealthy, you know.

"He said, 'For instance, to give you an idea: I bought a piece of land, in an area of Texas. I bought a small strip but very long; narrow but long. Well, here comes a power company that wants to build a power line, so they pay us for the use of the land. But all around here, my neighbors were cutting one corner here, another corner there, me—one foot inside my property. I didn't do that; I didn't plan any of that stuff. Here's another luxury.'

"Maybe he projected, mentally, about buying that piece of land. That's clairvoyance again.

"That's the kind of world we live in.

"So we are trying to control that part of it as best we can, and use it for establishing the path that we should follow, and to be sure we are on the correct path, and to improve it as we go," Silva added.

Going Beyond Hypnosis

Isabel is a natural psychic. Nobody taught her how.

But her father, José Silva, noticed some things that helped him devise a simple system to train anybody to do what Isabel was doing naturally.

She started exhibiting her psychic ability during a hypnosis session. When he analyzed the experience later on, he realized that she was not in the usual deep hypnosis level where subjects only function inductively, where they can take in information but cannot analyze it and solve problems.

Instead she was in a lighter level, a level between outer consciousness and hypnosis, similar to the level you are at when you first wake up in the morning. At this level she could function deductively as well as inductively. It is a level that psychologists call the subconscious.

At that level she could analyze information and make decisions and take action on her own. That is what she did when she spoke up and told her father what he wanted to know before he told her what he wanted to know.

That led him to modify the standard hypnosis method he had been using. Instead of taking people all the way to the depth where they could only function inductively, he stopped partway. You will learn to go to that level with the Silva Centering Exercise in Chapter 12.

Then he developed a system of "mental calisthenics" you can use to access the lifetime of psychic information that is stored on your right brain hemisphere and copy it to your left brain hemisphere so you can use it consciously whenever you need it. You will learn that in Part 3 of this book.

CHAPTER 2

Local ESP—Secrets of Charisma & Personal Power

Another "extra" sense, in addition to the so-called five physical senses of sight, sound, touch, taste, and smell, involves your body's aura. You have probably experienced it. Have you ever:

- Stared at somebody until they turn and look at you? Or perhaps you have been the one who was stared at.
- Met someone and known instantly that this is a person you like, and would become friends with?
- Met someone and known instantly that this is someone you don't like and cannot trust, and you turned out to be correct?
- Said something and your friend replied, "I was going to say that—you read my mind!"?

You need to verify because this "extra sense" is a two-way street. Just as you can get someone to react when you stare at them, any good con artist can use the physical part of their aura to urge you to trust them.

That only works when the con artist is within range of the physical part of your aura. From a distance, they cannot hide from your inquisitive mind. You will learn in Part 3 of this book how to project your mind to any point or place on the planet to get information and learn the truth when you need it.

Some people seem to be able to "see" auras by detecting a visible light around a person's body. But it is easier and more direct to just project your mind to any depth within the person's body or mind to get the information you need.

"Home Field Advantage" is real. It is about more than 100,000 sports fans making a lot of noise to distract the visiting team and make it hard for them to communicate with each other. A lot of those home fans will be picturing their team coming out on top.

Good actors and entertainers feed off the audience, and they project energy back to the audience. That's why we enjoy going to live events so much.

Some people seem to be able to impose their will on others with their thoughts, without saying or doing anything.

Even animals get in on the act. Every pet owner who has watched their dog jump up and run out of the room when they thought about giving it a bath knows what about that.

What Is the Aura?

We can measure various physical energies radiating from living things, including the human body. These include heat, odor, and brainwaves. Dogs can detect this energy and track us down long after we have left the area.

Humans can detect it too. You may have experienced this if you tried to sneak up on somebody quietly but they turned and saw you as you got close. Or perhaps you have "sensed" someone's mood even before they said anything.

Polygraph expert Cleve Backster was surprised one night when a plant in his office, a dragon tree, had a panic reaction to his intention to burn one of its leaves.

He recalled how that experience came about:

"For whatever reason, it occurred to me that it would be interesting to see how long it took water to get from the root area of a plant, all the way up the long trunk and out and down to the leaves," he said.

So he connected the galvanic skin response section of a polygraph onto a leaf of a dragon tree plant in his office, poured water into the pot, and sat back to watch and see what happened.

The plant reacted, but not the way Backster expected.

"The tracings on the printout had the contour of a human being tested," he said, "reacting the way a person does when you are asking a question that could get them in trouble.

"So I forgot about the rising water time and said to myself, 'Wow, this thing wants to show me people-like reactions.'

"So I began to wonder what I could do that would be a threat to the well-being of the plant, similar to the fact that a relevant question regarding a crime could be a threat to a person taking a polygraph test if they're lying."

Then the idea occurred to him that he could burn the plant.

"I didn't have matches in the room," he said. "I wasn't touching the plant in any way. I was maybe five feet away from the desk. I was essentially away from the plant.

"The only new thing that occurred was my intent to burn that plant leaf.

"In an instant, when I thought of burning that plant leaf and the image entered my mind, the polygraph went into a wild agitation.

"Now this was very late at night and towards morning. The building was empty and there was just no other reason for this reaction. I thought, *Wow! This thing read my mind!* It was that obvious to me right then, and my consciousness hasn't been the same since."

He continued to work with what he calls "primary perception" for the next 47 years. We will cover one of his experiments with human cells in Chapter 3.

There Are No Secrets from Psychics

Nothing can block your mind and stop you from sending good thoughts:

Good parents do the same with their children.

Effective business managers do it with the employees they manage.

Top salespeople communicate with their aura.

Our best friends are people we are attuned to.

Successful marriages involve a blending of auras.

You can read more about this in our book *Silva UltraMind's Persuasive Thoughts.*

José Silva even created a special technique so his children could use this "Local ESP" to get answers to test questions directly from their teacher even if they had missed class the day the topic was covered.

If you relax and enter the alpha level, it should be easy for you to get the answer directly from the instructor, as long as the instructor is within range of the physical part of your aura.

Once you have fully developed your ESP as you learn in Section 3 of this book, you can get answers from anybody anywhere, no matter how far away.

Now let's call on José Silva again to explain what he learned about the body's energy fields.

The Human Body's 7 Radiating Energy Fields
by José Silva

All energies radiate, because they're dynamic. There's some movement that causes energy to be dynamic, because static energy serves no purpose. It has to be in motion, at some level, to produce results.

So energy number one, pure spiritual energy, causes a radiation, and this radiation causes subatomic particles to start appearing.

Once energy number two is fully matured, it's called the subatomic dimension. It too is dynamic, it too radiates, and its radiation causes atoms to start forming.

Atoms radiate their own energy. The sum total of all atoms is called the atomic dimension.

We call them subjective dimensions because they cannot be perceived with biological senses: sight, hearing, touch, smell, taste.

Dimension number two is the subatomic. Number three is atomic.

We need to keep in mind that energy number one doesn't belong to us. It's a fundamental energy brought from another dimension that we cannot perceive, or even fathom what that can be.

We cannot alter the first energy field. We can alter all the others, but we need to have human intelligence to do so.

So then dimension number one is pure spiritual energy, number two is subatomic, and number three is atomic.

The atomic radiation causes molecules to start appearing, and it's called the molecular dimension. It too is dynamic, in a sense, because it radiates energy. This is the fourth dimension, the molecular dimension.

We're not talking about Einstein, physical objective dimensions. We're talking about our subjective dimensions, the non-physical world of the mind.

From molecular on down, we have the subjective. And from molecular on forward, we start having objective.

From molecular, in the center, we start forming inanimate matter, everything that we know to be inanimate: metals, rocks, and so on.

Next we develop animate matter. Cells start appearing because of the dynamic fourth dimension, plus the energies of the pure number one, number two, number three. All combined, the energy radiations cause cells to appear, and when cells appear, it's called the cellular dimension.

Now we have life: plants, animals, organs, and organ systems.

7: Organ systems

6: Organs

5: Cells

4: Molecules

3: Atoms

2: Subatomic particles

1: Pure spiritual energy

The Highest Form of Life on the Planet

Now the human brain starts appearing on the scene.

We have two different kinds of brain cells. By kinds, we mean cells that become resonant with one another. There are two different forms of resonance. By resonance, we mean in harmony, in attunement. Many of the cells come together and function as one. So the opposing factors that control the function of cells are minimal, and that's called the impedance that hinders the movement of currents. All these cells are like battery cells; they can be charged and discharged.

Cells are going to develop brain matter to produce objective matter and subjective matter, which exist in two different dimensions.

Animals exist in the objective and subjective.

Plants exist in the objective and subjective.

In the human brain, some cells become resonant in harmony with one another to produce the objective concept.

Other cells become resonant, and besides being objective and subjective, they have a third factor called spiritual.

The animal brain does not have that.

All animal brains—both brain hemispheres—are objective and subjective, period.

But the human brain has objective-subjective left brain hemisphere and objective-subjective right brain hemisphere, plus the spiritual component.

The spiritual component is what distinguishes the human being from an animal.

There's nothing higher than us here on planet Earth. We are the superior life form. My concept is that we were sent here by a power higher than us with the responsibility and the power to correct problems and convert the planet into a paradise.

There's nothing we cannot do, and there's no place where the mind cannot go. Think about it and you're there.

CHAPTER 3

Maternal ESP, a Special Bond Every Mother Has

Every mother has a strong psychic bond with her children. This is true no matter the child's age or how far away they are.

There have been many anecdotal reports of mothers experiencing a sudden fear and learning later that their child was in trouble or had been injured or died at that exact time.

Here is an example from David Aretha, editor of this book: "My mom's friend's sister felt a powerful shock through her body. At that moment, in another house, her son was electrocuted while taking a bath when a TV fell into the bathtub."

There have also been controlled scientific experiments verifying this automatic connection between mother and child.

One of the first to be widely reported was conducted in the Soviet Union in the 1950s but not reported publicly until twenty years later.

The United States government's Central Intelligence Agency (CIA) wrote about this research in a report that was declassified in 2001 in response to a Freedom of Information Act (FOIA) request:

"Soviet researcher Paul Naumov described an experiment where a mother rabbit was placed in a laboratory with electrodes implanted in her brain to monitor activity.

"Her baby rabbits were taken aboard a submarine which then submerged deep in the ocean.

"At synchronized times the baby rabbits were killed and at each precise moment the mother rabbit's brain reacted.

"This innate form of communication which traversed great distance and ocean depths may be the source of many 'natural instincts.'"

How a Mother Solved a Longstanding Problem

José Silva conducted his own experiment testing the mother-child psychic connection in the early 1960s, before he knew about the Soviet research. It involved a child who was wetting the bed every night.

He asked the child's mother to send her son to another city 150 miles away, and to stay there with relatives for a full month. Then he told the mother to "program" her child every night, a half hour after his bedtime.

The first night, she closed her eyes and imagined that when her son felt pressure in his tummy and needed to use the bathroom, he would awaken, get up, go to the bathroom, urinate, then go back to bed and go back to sleep. She mentally pictured all of this, like making a "mental movie."

Silva had cautioned her not to call her son or the relatives he was staying with because he did not want to contaminate his experiment. But she called anyway, the next day. She didn't mention the bed wetting—but the relative did. "His bed was dry this morning!" the relative told her.

And he never wet the bed again.

They solved the problem in just one night with Maternal ESP.

This phenomenon works "because the child was once part of the mother," Silva said.

Then Silva tried another experiment to confirm his hypothesis that you cannot harm a person with your mind from a distance.

He asked some experienced psychics to enter their clairvoyant level during the night, project to the child mentally, and see if they could influence him to wet the bed again.

They tried for several nights, but the youngster never wet the bed again.

Communication at the Cell Level

If we can communicate mentally with plants, can we also communicate directly with our own body cells? Researcher Cleve Backster put that question to the test and got some very interesting answers.

His research helps us understand why mothers have such powerful psychic bonds with their offspring.

His experiments with white cells from human donors provides more insight and confirmation of the Soviet research with the mother rabbit and her cubs, and why mothers are psychically attuned to their offspring.

How Negative Thoughts Can Damage
Your Immune System

The following is transcribed from a presentation by Cleve Backster at a Silva convention in 1995:

"These white cells are so instrumental in the immune system that they are very important," Backster said.

"The work that we've done in hundreds of hours of testing of the white cells is just absolutely fascinating.

"There's no doubt about it that your thoughts can permeate every cell of your body, without going through any of the conventional communications systems.

"In other words, if your thoughts, when your cells are separated from your body and being tested, under glass or in vitro, if they can react to your emotions when you are separated from them, you know in your body that they are going to react to emotional changes, particularly the negative emotions.

"The problem is, nothing is quite as disruptive as negative thinking.

"We use negative thinking to see these reactions when they do occur.

"The positive stuff you don't see. It shows free flowing changes on the chart.

"But the negative stuff, right away you see these bursts of electrical activity from the cells that have been separated from the donor.

"So it means that when you are thinking negative thoughts, you are not doing yourself any favor. This would certainly bear that out.

"The Silva Mind training, all the way through, is always talking about the quality of your thoughts, the positive thinking, better and better. This is so important. And it does have a scientific basis . . . there is no doubt about it whatsoever.

"The next slide is an example of the first time when I got the technology of how to collect these cells—these are my own white cells that I'd collected, and I'd bought myself a centrifuge and whatever I needed to do this work.

"Here I was going through a shelf and looking for some little sterile lancets. I wanted to cut my hand just a little bit with these sterile lancets and put some iodine in there because I'd always been able to get good reactions with plants when I did that.

"Here is the thought of doing this. While I was looking on the shelf for the lancets, it caused this reaction here. Not when I did it, because the cells were prepared; it wasn't spontaneous. It was spontaneous as I thought about doing this and was looking for these lancets on the shelf.

"You can see the size: these are not subtle reactions, these are huge reactions.

"So this was my first experience with the white cells, and it started a whole bunch of white cell testing that grew to be very important.

"For instance, in one experiment a leukocyte cell sample taken from the mouth of a donor was hooked up to EEG instrumentation. Later, after the donor had returned home (15 miles away), a deflection was noted on the polygraph and the timing of it was matched against what the donor reported doing at that time: watching a program entitled "World at War."

"The donor's in vitro white cells in our lab reacted to the downing of the enemy aircraft on the television program.

"Experiments like this demonstrated that we communicate with cells from our own body even if they are far removed from our body," Backster concluded.

How to Use Maternal ESP

José Silva's research confirmed that all mothers can use this ability to help their children. The mother does not have to be a Silva graduate or know how to enter the alpha level in order to do this, but it helps. Here is how to proceed:

Wait until your child has been asleep for at least a half an hour. Then relax, visualize your child, and then you can communicate with your child on a deep inner level, where the child will not reject your advice and guidance.

Whatever you do must be in the child's best interest, something that the child will benefit from doing.

Identify behavior that you want to change, and then program your child in this manner. The father can do it too, but in order to do this, the father must know how to enter the alpha level, then activate his mind—become mentally active—and remain at the alpha level while doing his programming. You can learn this in Part 3 of this Master Course.

When there are many problems, try starting with the smallest problem first. When you correct that one, then go to the next most serious problem. If your results are satisfactory, then continue in this same manner.

If you are not satisfied with your results starting with the smallest problem, then do just the opposite: Program the most serious problem, the most important one. Think of all the reasons you want to correct this problem, all of the benefits. Think of how many people will benefit in addition to your child and you. The more people who will benefit, the more desire you will have, and this will help you to get much better results.

Teach Your Child to Function as a Genius

You can also guide the child to correct the problem. When they are six, it is easy to teach them to enter the alpha level and help themself.

Tell them to relax—first thing in the morning would be a great time. Then go to work on one specific problem. Start with the smallest problem. For instance, if there is something she does that you want them to change—to do differently—then call their attention to the behavior you desire to change. Then tell them to erase that mental picture and replace it with one doing what you believe would be better for them.

Start by programming them, at night, while they sleep, as outlined above. You can tell them mentally that you are going to give them a way to do things mentally, so that they will be happier, healthier, and more successful. If you do this with love, and desire, then you will get great results.

There are detailed instructions in the book *Create a Genius* by José and Robert Stone.

Now let's hear from José Silva himself with more information.

How to Solve Problems
by José Silva

Sons and daughters are like an extension of their mother's body at another dimension, at the subjective dimension. Not biologically—subjectively.

The mother is in a position to program the child anytime she pleases. Even if the child is eighty years old, she can still program him if she wants to, if she knows how to go this level and program through visualization and imagination.

The mother is more spiritual and is a proper programmer for the child. She has tremendous programming influence of the child regardless of whether the child likes it or not.

The Knowledge of Those Who Came Before

We find that our teenage generation will sometimes fight that. "What right does my mother have to program me? I have my own life to live." Let's look into that.

We all have our own lives to live. Whoever got here first experiments and collects information and passes it on to the newcomers.

Then we do the same thing for those that come after us. We test out the information, we add, we subtract, and we condense it and give it to the ones who come after. This is education. We don't have to go through hundreds and thousands of years of collecting information for education. We get a condensed version from the ones who came before us.

Now, who would you think, even if you believe it or not, would have more desire to help you than anybody else?

Your mother.

Whatever she does, right or wrong, error or not, she has the right to do that. And she has the means, whether we like it or not, because of the bond between the mother and child. It's the mother who doesn't know that she can program, who sometimes fails in doing so in this manner.

She can project, she can solve many problems for her offspring, if she knew how to do it, by entering this dimension. We say this is the way it should be, we think.

Mothers are learning to be more spiritual than ever before because they're developing the ability to project into the subjective dimension and to project into the future of their offspring and to figure out what they're getting into.

Whoever Gets There First Wins

It's a lot easier to program your children before somebody else does. The problem was that most parents couldn't project far enough ahead to determine whether their child was getting into trouble or not.

Once somebody else programs them, then we have a dual problem: The deconditioning for one and reconditioning for another. Deprogramming and reprogramming.

If someone down the street programs your son or daughter before you do, then you've got a problem. Because then you have to deprogram that and then reprogram something else in its place. It's more difficult.

If you get there first, it's ideal. We say: Mothers, get there first.

If the mother, when she was talking to her infant baby or singing a lullaby to the baby, putting them to sleep, if she would have said at the time: "You will never smoke, you will never drink, you will never ..."

That is effective even if the child is only three or four months old. When they get to the age where somebody urges them to try smoking or drinking, mother's programming is already impressed and it takes effect then.

How to Deprogram a Problem

Deprogramming is more complex than programming. If mother can guide her teenager to the alpha level, it is relatively easy to do.

If the son or daughter is not going to allow their mother to work like that with them, then she's going to handle it subjectively within the reach of the physical part of the aura, but at the subjective level.

Once she is at the alpha level to program the child, she visualizes the child as though the child is right there with her, and then she talks to the child, never scolding, never forcing anything.

"Son or daughter, this is what's going on. There's a difference in opinion here. There's a difference of understanding. Something is wrong with our communication. I'm trying to do this for you. I would like to do this for you. You seem to be rejecting . . ." whatever. Do it like this.

Then you can even put words in his or her mouth to accept this kind of communication in harmony with what your understanding is and so forth.

He says, "I'm sorry. What happened? I'm sorry, Ma." Act as if it took place and take things for granted.

Enter your alpha level and to say these things to him or to her and then watch for them to start changing completely, being more receptive, and so forth.

How to Stop a Child's Bed Wetting

What the mother needs to do is visualize her child when they wet the bed, wets it every night. She can be at a distance. You don't have to be in the same environment. Visualize this child where they sleep and the way they look when they have done their thing, wetting the bed, whatever.

Then imagine the child with a bladder full, who needs to go to the bathroom.

Imagine the child opening their eyes, sitting up in bed and walking step by step. Imagine them walking until they get to the bathroom. Imagine them doing what they need to do. Imagine them walking again until standing by the bed, sitting by the bed, placing head on pillow, eyes closed and back to sleep. In the morning, very happy because the bed is clean and dry.

That's it. This is done subjectively.

A hypnotist can do it objectively by taking the child to this level, touching their bladder and telling them, "When you feel it is full and that you need to go to the bathroom, you will open your eyes. Your eyes will open. You will sit up in bed. You will stand up by the bed. You will walk." The hypnotist tells them step by step what to do.

"Go straight to the bathroom, then after you are finished, walk backward, back again towards the bed. Stand by the bed. You will sit on the bed. You'll place head on pillow, you will close eyes.

"In the morning, you're going to wake up very happy because your bed is clean and dry."

Hypnotists never say, "Do not wet your bed." They never mention wetting the bed. It works objectively. With hypnosis, you can alter the involuntary nervous system to act opposing for nature. This is why it's dangerous to be hypnotized by an amateur who doesn't know what he's doing.

CHAPTER 4

Assisted ESP—Dowsing, Pendulums, etc.

During his twenty-two years of scientific research into the mind and human potential, José Silva investigated everything that he came across that seemed like it might help people learn to actually use the untapped power of the mind to solve more problems and achieve successful outcomes.

He investigated fortune telling, crystal ball gazing, tarot cards, pendulums, Ouija boards, dowsing rods, channeling, astral projection, reincarnation, astrology, numerology, and more.

He studied hypnosis, he assisted faith healers, he learned and practiced the techniques of the Rosicrucians, and more. He saw people who were benefiting from these techniques. He learned what they did and why they did it.

During all this study and research, he stripped away the mystery and showmanship and uncovered the underlying principles that all of those techniques rely on.

What did he learn, and why did he select only certain techniques to include in his Silva UltraMind ESP System?

Let's walk with him through some of the research he did, learn what he learned, and evaluate it from his point of view.

Some "Psychic" Devices Evaluated

Some devices, like dowsing rods and pendulums, can reveal Local ESP.

Other methods, like crystal balls, channeling, automatic writing, spirit guides, palm reading, Taro cards, and astral projection, provide an intermediate step for natural psychics to tap into their ESP.

The Ideomotor Response to Psychic Messages

Your thoughts affect your body. You think of someone you love and you smile. When you are thirsty you don't even need to think about what to do; you just reach for a glass of water and drink it.

The term combines "ideo" (idea) and "motor" (movement), highlighting the link between mental activity and automatic, unconscious physical action, movements triggered by thoughts, ideas, or mental images, rather than by deliberate intention.

Or as we like to say: Mind guides brain and brain guides body.

Remote Ideomotor Response

Your thoughts can also affect tissue that used to be part of your body even if the tissue is far away. You saw that in the Soviet research with the mother rabbit and her babies in Chapter 2.

Another example is the mother who programmed her child to stop wetting the bed. The child, who was in another city, received the message and carried out the instructions even though he was not consciously aware of it.

More Kinds of Assisted ESP

Without training, most people are not aware of the psychic information they detect. There are several ways you can get a "notification" when a message has arrived, including: dowsing rods, pendulums, Ouija boards, automatic writing (and typing), dreams, and electronic equipment like brain wave sensors and galvanic skin response devices.

Trained psychics don't need to wait and depend on devices to help them because previously they identified points of reference in the subjective (mental) dimension that help them quickly recognize and identify psychic information. Any information they can access with devices or spirit guides or dreams they can also access mentally on-demand so they can deal with problems immediately.

Traditional scientists dismiss the possibility of ESP being involved, saying there is no logical basis and it is only the person's subconscious thoughts and memories that cause a reaction. But sometimes the information received is beyond anything the person has ever had physical contact with, so we respectfully disagree with those scientists who don't admit that we might actually know something they don't know yet.

Experiences of a Self-Taught Dowser

Raymon Grace has been a lot of things in his life including: carpenter, dowser, holistic faith healer, Silva instructor, and humanitarian.

"There is nothing magical about dowsing," Grace says, "and there is no power in the instrument used. The power is in the human mind and dowsing helps focus the mind.

"Dowsing is simply the use of a physical object that tells us what we already know but don't realize we know it.

"Some believe that dowsing is a 'gift' and you either have it or you don't. While some people have a natural ability for dowsing, as some have a natural ability for art, music, or various skills, dowsing is a teachable skill," he explained.

"I know, because I observed other dowsers, asked questions, practiced, and taught myself how to do it." Now he encourages other people to use dowsing to improve their lives, and they report many successes.

"If we have better information, we can make better decisions, and dowsing is a way to get that information," Grace explained.

"If you wonder where the information comes from, I would say it comes from the same place as an intuitive thought that helps you solve a problem.

"We have evidence that dowsing has been successful in many ways including:
- lowering violence in schools
- bringing about compatibility in family and business
- changing the effect of food on the body
- improving water and improving the health of people and animals
- reducing abuse on women and children
- made more money
- experienced a sense of personal empowerment

"If the emails folks write me are true, we are making good progress in all of these areas."

Obviously you will get even better results after you complete the Silva ESP training in Section 3 of this book or with the Silva UltraMind ESP System Complete Home Seminar or a live Silva ESP training course.

You can learn more about Raymon and his work in his books and on his RaymonGrace.us website.

Now let's take a look at how to use dowsing rods and other aids to show you what your mind already knows.

Easily Make Your Own Dowsing Rods

Dowsers use several types of devices for dowsing, most commonly forked twigs, L-shaped rods, or pendulums.

There are photos and videos on many websites including RaymonGrace.us and Pinterest.com of how to make dowsing rods. But beware of outlandish claims that you can "manifest" wealth just by using them. Remember: Nothing is free. Everything is paid for by somebody.

You can make a set of L-shaped dowsing rods in a minute or two from a couple of wire coat hangers:

First straighten them out, then bend one end to a 90-degree angle, an "L" shape. The short end should be long enough to hold comfortably in your hand. The other end will be a lot longer, and that means the long end will move to one side or the other with the least effort.

To use them, hold the rods lightly so that they will sway back and forth easily. Then point them straight ahead and walk around with them until they react. Keep an image in mind of what you are looking for.

How to Make and Use a Pendulum

Pendulums are quite popular too. You can make one by simply attaching a small weight to a string. The weight can be a crystal or small piece of metal, and you can attach it to a necklace if you wish. Raymon Grace uses a small metal weight on a chain.

For my first experiments with a pendulum, I just tied some old keys to the end of a string. It worked great. It helped me improve my accuracy in working health detection and correction cases, which we will cover in Chapter 21.

Here is how you can calibrate your pendulum:

Sit down, relax, and enter your level. Hold the end of the chain with your dominant hand, with your elbow resting on a table. The crystal should hang just above the tabletop and have little or no movement.

Then desire for the pendulum to show you "Yes," and let it move. Typically, it will swing forward and back or side to side or in a circle. Then ask it for other answers. The responses for me were:

Yes: Forward and back.

No: Side to side.

Maybe: Clockwise.

I don't know: Counter-clockwise.

Now you can ask it any question and expect one of those answers.

A pendulum is also useful for "map dowsing." People have used pendulums to find the best spots to look for water, oil, and precious metals like silver and gold. They move the pendulum around over a map of their property, and when it reacts they know where to drill. You can also walk around the property while holding the pendulum and thinking about what you want to find and let it react.

A Quick Way to Verify Your Dowsing Ability

Back when I was brand new at this, there was a Silva graduate who loved dowsing rods, and he insisted I try them. He handed me a pair and told me to walk across his yard, in front of his house, and desire to find the main pipe carrying water into his house.

As I got to the concrete walkway from the street to his front door, the dowsing rods reacted. I didn't think that could be right because that would mean the pipe was buried beneath the concrete walkway, or right next to it.

He said that was exactly where the pipe was. He told me to go to the street and look for the water meter at the edge of his yard. Sure enough, there was the water meter, exactly in line with the walkway.

You can search for anything. Another friend of mine invited me to go on an archaeological dig with him and a group of people at an "Indian mound," which was described to me as a place where Native Americans had buried their garbage.

I used dowsing rods to see if they could help me find the best place to dig. They did, and they produced the second-best find of the day, a well-preserved hip bone from a huge animal.

Dowsing for Dollars

With the first UltraMind ESP System that José Silva taught, he included a dowsing demonstration. Jose Luis "Pepe" Romero, one of the three people José Silva selected to launch the new Silva UltraMind ESP System in 1998, was assisting and recalled what happened.

Mr. Silva hid an envelope with some money somewhere in the classroom. When the students came back from break, he gave Romero a set of dowsing rods and told him to walk around the room and let the dowsing rods guide him to the money. Romero told us later that even before he used the dowsing rods he knew where the money was, but he didn't say anything and let the dowsing rods guide him to the money.

"If you can find it, you can have it," he told him.

Romero said he already knew where the money was at that point, but he used the dowsing rods anyway and walked all around the room, and when he got close to where he thought the money was, the dowsing rods did their thing and, as expected, he found the envelope with the money.

The dowsing rods are like biofeedback equipment: Mind guides brain; brain activates little muscles. Those dowsing rods take so little to cause them to move. We're not even aware that we're twitching or anything like that and they're moving.

The demonstration went well, but Silva decided to use psychometry in the course instead of the dowsing rods.

More Ideomotor Instruments

There are many other instruments and strategies that use the same ideomotor response mechanism as dowsing rods.

Ouija Boards have been around since the late nineteenth century. To some people they are a fun game. Others consider them a great way to obtain information. And some people are afraid of them because they don't understand them.

The Ouija Board has all of the letters of the alphabet printed on it as well as the words Yes, No, and Goodbye. To use it you place your fingers on a small movable pointer, close your eyes, and let the pointer move around the board to reveal the answer to the question you have in mind. Two people can put their fingers on the pointer if you wish.

Channeling and **Spirit Guides** can also reveal hidden information to believers. Even if you don't believe you have the ability to detect the information on your own, if you believe that somebody else can, then you imagine asking them. It is still the same ideomotor response, revealing what you already know but don't realize that you know.

José Silva even used a variation of this in the original Silva Mind Control course. Some of the children he was working with felt so small and helpless when communicating mentally with adults that he had them create two imaginary helpers, a man and a woman.

As they grew older and more confident, they relied less and less on their imaginary helpers until they didn't need them anymore.

Some grownups also had trouble believing that they had the ability to project their mind anywhere in the universe to get information that would help them solve problems.

I was one of those people when I took the course back in 1975, and I used my imaginary helpers a lot. Then one day after a decade of teaching the course and several years working for José Silva at his Laredo headquarters, a lady called the office and told me that some of the Silva graduates where she lived had told her that José Silva said that those imaginary helpers would eventually fade away because you didn't need them anymore.

I told her I had never heard that, and I hoped they were mistaken. He was in the office, so I told her I would go ask him. I called her back and told her he'd confirmed it, and over the next couple of years I weaned myself off that technique.

Astral Projection is a technique that you can use to go directly to the source of the information you need. You imagine that your "astral body" leaves your physical body and goes wherever you direct it to go.

A British researcher named Alexander Canon set up a research project to prove the reality of astral projection. He worked with four subjects:

In one room, he had a man and a woman.

In another location, at a distant point, he had a man (let's call him M), and in a third location, he had a woman (we will call her F).

He asked subjects M and F, who were each by themselves, to each project their astral body to the room where the man and woman were together, and to report what they saw.

The man, subject M, said that he saw three people: one man and two women.

The woman, subject F, said that she saw three people: two men and one woman.

This, said Cannon, proved astral projection.

José Silva had an idea about mental projection, and he set out to demonstrate it with the following experiment. Here it is in his own words:

Our Mental Projection Experiment

by José Silva

I was working with an assistant. I told him that I would stay at my house, and he could go to the shop, the television repair shop next door to the house. We could see each other through the windows, and could signal to each other.

We were working with two young boys. I wanted to get my subject to level first, then have my assistant get his subject to check out my subject, to find out what was going on. When we were ready, I told my subject to enter his level. Then I told him, "We want to create something."

He said, "What's that?"

I said, "To have something for the first time, you know, something that's not around. Something that we don't have around. For instance, I don't want you to think about your father's car, or your uncle's car. I want you to create a car, any way you want to, in your mind. Just like make-believe."

He said, "Just like make-believe? Okay." Then he continued, "I'm going to create a little toy truck. How's that?"

I said, "That's fine."

"Now, where do I start?" he asked.

I said, "Wherever you want to start."

He said, "Well, I'm going to start with the front wheels first. I'm imagining that here's the front wheels, here's the axle connecting one wheel to the other."

He kept on like that. And he said, "I am going to paint it green with red wheels."

When he was doing this, I signaled to my assistant, through the window, to start. So he told the other boy, "Will you project to see what little Johnny is doing?"

"He is creating a little toy truck," the second boy answered, and he described it.

Then he added, "He is going to paint it green with red wheels."

Thoughts Are Things in the Subjective Dimension

This could be what happened in Cannon's astral projection experiment. The man and the woman both imagined that their astral bodies were in the room with the other subjects.

They might have been creating images of their bodies, in another dimension, the same way Johnny created the little toy truck in another dimension.

In other words, that is an alternate explanation for astral projection. But we know we can have mental projection, and that you can create something with your mind in another dimension, and someone else who is functioning in that same dimension can detect it and describe it.

The little toy truck only existed subjectively; there was no physical truck. And the second boy had accurately detected the first boy's intention to paint it green with red wheels.

That doesn't disprove astral projection, but it does offer a viable alternative to the theory of astral bodies.

Even more important, think of the value of being able to detect another person's intentions:

Parents can know what their children are planning before they do it and take steps to keep them from getting into trouble.

Business managers can know the intentions of their customers, as well as their employees, suppliers, investors, government regulators, and more.

Nobody will be able to start a war because they cannot block others from detecting their intentions.

Travel Mentally Through Time

Age regression means projecting yourself back in time, to study aspects of your youth that you might not recall consciously, and even further: With prenatal age regression you can go back to a time before you were born.

The concept of reincarnation suggests that we live more than just one lifetime on the planet. A hypnotist can age-regress a subject back to their birth and then beyond, sometimes hundreds or even thousands of years prior to their birth into this current lifetime.

When José Silva regressed his nine-year-old daughter to a time before her birth, she said she lived in Paris, so he called on a local priest who had lived in Paris to help him. The priest asked the girl, while she was in a hypnotic state, some questions about the city and she answered correctly even though she had never been to Paris.

When her father asked the "Parisian woman" what her favorite recipe was, she replied "duck a l'orange," and she described it. Silva wrote down exactly what she'd said.

At that time there was a French chef working in a Laredo restaurant, so after the session was over they went to the restaurant and asked the chef if the recipe was real. He confirmed it, and added that one feature involved using a utensil that had been used in the past but most people no longer used.

Silva said this experience could indicate that the girl had actually lived before, or there could be another explanation: a "floating mind." She might have projected her mind to the priest and detected the information her father was asking for. It would be kind of like having the answers to a test ahead of time.

And perhaps she had heard that there was a French chef in Laredo so when she was asked for her favorite recipe she could have projected her mind to the French chef and gotten the answers from him.

It was experiences like these that convinced José Silva that the mind could get information directly.

Even though he saw people getting information through reincarnation experiences, astral projection, card reading, crystal balls, pendulums, dowsing rods, astrology, numerology, Ouija boards, channeling, and so forth, he found that his subjects could get all the information they needed in order to solve problems by using mental projection.

Silva's own children, and the other subjects he was working with, were getting information directly with their minds. They were working health cases, detecting information with the mind and then verifying that it was accurate.

Why, Silva wondered, go to all the trouble of using those other tools, and run the risk of making a mistake, when you could obtain information directly with your mind, and then use that information to correct problems?

Research Debunks the Evil Spirit Myth

The idea of evil spirits is a concern for some people, and some religions warn against using these devices and strategies out of fear they might provide a way for an "evil spirit" to enter the person.

José Silva's research with the child who wet the bed, reported in Chapter 3, debunked those ancient warnings when trained psychics couldn't get the child to start wetting the bed again.

How to Counteract Negative Thoughts

If someone you know has been subjected to negative thoughts, there are ways you can help them neutralize those thoughts and fears.

An experience José Silva had with his own children led to an easy way to deal with unwanted thoughts:

A babysitter wanted his children to stay in bed, so she told them, "There is a monster under your bed, and if you get out of bed the monster will eat you up alive!"

When José and Paula Silva returned home later that evening they learned what had happened. The children were afraid to get out of bed to go to the bathroom.

So he took their children to the alpha level and told them that whenever they saw a monster, to "point at it and shake your finger, and every time you shake your finger at the monster it will get smaller and smaller and smaller until it is so small you can hold it in your hand and then it can't hurt you at all."

Knowledge, When Applied, Is Power

I ran my own experiment about a year after I graduated from the Silva Mind Control course. There was a man who said he was a natural psychic and he could put any thought into my head at any time and he could do it from a distance. He said that if he wanted me to think of a certain color I would, and there wasn't anything I could do to block him.

I didn't think he could, so I asked him if he would be willing to demonstrate that to me and he agreed. I told him I would not do anything to block him and he was happy with that. I never saw him or heard from him again, physically or mentally.

Why "Evil Spirits" Cannot Harm You Physically

Later, after I came to work at Silva headquarters in Laredo, Texas, I learned that José Silva took a similar approach.

The "Brujas" who practiced their brand of witchcraft here on the Mexican-American border didn't want him teaching people that Brujas can't harm them mentally so they used their tactics against him.

He didn't do anything to try to stop them. He just ignored them, so they concluded that he was more powerful than they were and decided to leave him alone.

Spirit guides, evil spirits, ghosts, and similar concepts are our own creations, like the little toy truck. And there is no more risk of any of them harming you than there is in getting run over by that little toy truck that the child created with his mind.

Why? Because mental creations cannot use force. Only something physical can apply physical force. Subjective we correct by attraction; physically we correct by repulsion.

If someone has a malfunctioning heart, the doctor can use physical means to correct it, while psychics visualizes and imagines a perfect organ to attract it back to the form, the blueprint, that the Creator intended.

All of those are ways of using your mind to get information, correct abnormalities, and create beneficial solutions that are best for everybody involved.

Performing an Exorcism When Other People Failed

José Silva was a very pragmatic problem-solver who would work within another person's belief system to correct a serious problem if that's what was necessary.

Here is an example of an instance when he worked within another person's belief system to correct a serious problem. It was during a trip to Venezuela to present his Ultra Seminar. Someone told him about a young woman who was "possessed" by an "evil spirit," and nobody had been able to help her. They asked if he could help her.

He agreed, and they took him to the young woman.

When he arrived, she was acting out—out of control. She wouldn't respond to anyone, but was crying and shouting and thrashing around.

Silva did not believe that there are evil entities that can harm us, and his research had confirmed it.

But the young woman, and the people with her, believed that she was possessed by an evil spirit. So in order to correct the problem, he had to work within her belief system.

First he had to get her to listen to him. And he needed for her to believe that he was powerful enough to help her. So he took care of both items at the same time:

He grabbed her by the wrist, and began to squeeze very tight. Mr. Silva was a strong man; he had been a prizefighter when he was young and had very large hands and arms.

So before long, his strong grip on her wrist started to become painful, not enough to harm her, just enough to get her attention. He told her, "That doesn't hurt. does it?" She replied. "Yes, it hurts!" Now they were communicating, so he could work with her.

He told her that he was there to help her, that her body had been taken over by an evil spirit, and that she wasn't strong enough by herself to fight it off, but that he was stronger and more powerful than the evil entity so that he would help her by positioning himself between her and the evil entity, and then the only way the evil entity could get to her was through him, and since he was more powerful, that wasn't going to happen.

Of course, he didn't believe that there was an evil entity, and therefore he didn't do anything to "block" such an "entity."

Instead, he programmed for her to believe him, and to accept what he said, because he knew that if she would do that, she would correct her own problem.

That is exactly what happened. She had felt José Silva's power herself—her sore wrist reminded her of that. So she believed him, believed that he was powerful enough to fight off the "evil spirit" that had possessed her.

The problem was solved, and everyone was happy.

More Devices Natural Psychics Use

There are other ways to reveal information. Devices like crystal balls, tarot cards, tea leaves, and palm reading are ways to help natural psychics focus their attention inward so they can become aware of what they know.

An astrologer who had taken the Silva ESP training told us that most of the information she gives to clients comes from her intuition and not from the alignment of the stars.

Use Your Ability to Solve Problems

Let's say you want to find something: a lost object, a job opening, a business opportunity, the source of pain in someone's body, a soul mate, a lost child, a new idea, or anything else.

You can let dowsing rods guide you, or a spirit guide can give you guidance. A pendulum or Ouija Board can show you what to do next. You can use astral projection to travel subjectively to the place where your answer is—or you could use mental projection and just project your mind to the information you need, and then take appropriate action both mentally and physically.

Mental projection is also the most scientifically valid. You could think of it as "Mind Dowsing," and you can enhance it with an advanced technique that you will learn in Chapter 33, the 3-Fingers Technique for Enhanced Intuition.

Dreams Can Bring Valuable Information

Dreams are often like postcards from your subconscious.

They can also be messages from higher intelligence if you have not developed another method like the MentalVideo, which we explain in Chapter 7.

Sometimes the dreams we have are not our own. Researchers found that people can influence other people's dreams when the dreamer is in a high alpha state. You can learn more in the book *Dream Telepathy* by Kripner and Ullman.

Clancy McKenzie, MD, a psychiatrist and longtime consultant to José Silva, has written extensively about how his dreams and his patients' dreams have led to medical breakthroughs and healing.

CHAPTER 5

Transportable ESP—Extend Your Reach

In Chapter 2 we discussed how the body's 7 radiating energy fields can alter things they come in contact with. This is similar to the way that information can be stored on a computer hard drive or on a "thumb drive" that you can carry in your pocket.

You can use a technique called psychometry to retrieve this stored information.

Here is how it works:

First obtain an item that the person has had in their presence for a long time. Then hold it in your left hand, enter the alpha level (you can learn how in Chapter 12), and desire to learn about this person: their physical characteristics (height, weight, hair color, age, health, etc.), if they are married and have children, their occupation and hobbies, are they happy and satisfied with their life, and whatever else you need to know about them.

There are detailed instructions in Chapter 19 as part of the Silva UltraMind ESP System training.

Using Psychometry to Influence People

In addition to using psychometry to obtain information about other people, you can also use it to send information to other people to help them in many ways:

- recover from health problems
- overcome bad habits and develop good new habits
- develop empathy
- become more confident and successful
- and other beneficial characteristics

Some religions use this same idea with "prayer beads" or other objects.

An Effective Crime-Fighting Tool

Several years ago longtime Silva instructor JoNell Monaco Lytle was volunteering her time to teach the Silva techniques to homeless people in Baltimore, Maryland. Forty-nine had signed up for the class.

Everything was going extremely well until the third day.

"Wednesday morning when I started to get into my van to drive to the class, I noticed the window was broken," JoNell said. "When I looked in, I saw that my van was mostly empty.

"Almost all of my Silva materials for the class were gone, including a large suitcase with books written and signed by José Silva.

"I wanted to cry."

There was a large rock on the seat on the passenger side. She took it with her to class and asked the students to sit around a large table.

"Even though I had not taught them any psychometry, I told them to go to level and mentally project into the rock and write down their impressions." she said.

"A number of us were able to describe what the person was wearing, all the way down to the kind of shoes he had on.

"Several people came up with the name of a street, the same street. Several came up with another street, and one had written down the intersection of the two streets.

"Three more homeless walked in just as we were finishing up the exercise. When we related the story, they made an about-face and off they went on foot, before I could stop them."

They returned a couple of hours later "with my Silva suitcase!

"The books were missing, and a lot of what I got back was damaged. They found some of it in the street and some of it was in trash cans and dumpsters.

"We celebrated.

"The thing we celebrated the most was how they had used their faculties of genius so effectively with so little Silva training behind them. They were all so proud."

JoNell tells the whole story about that class in our book *The Silva UltraMind ESP System.*

Programmed Water

One of the best materials for storing this kind of information is water. That's why you see priests and healers bless water, and why your mother feeds you chicken soup when you are sick.

One ounce of water contains 987 sextillion water molecules—which can also be written as 987 followed by 21 zeros.

Imagine what a powerful computer that would be. Imagine what you can accomplish if your thoughts can make just one change in a few million of those molecules.

Many scientists support the idea that our thoughts can cause a change in the physical characteristics of water and that this "programmed water" can promote faster healing and growth in both animals and plants.

One of these scientists is Dr. Bernard Grad. Here are highlights of a report he presented at a conference, "The Mind In Search of Itself," in 1972. It was cosponsored by Mind Science Foundation and Silva Mind Control International Inc. Here are some of the highlights of his report.

Even Untrained People Can Program Water

"This all started," Dr. Grad explained, "when a Hungarian gentleman (Mr. E.) came to me with the claim to be able to accelerate healing in people according to his experience in Hungary. I told him I was a biologist and therefore I couldn't bring any patients to him, but we could do experiments on animals and on plants."

They started by working with three groups of mice:

A control group with no treatment

A control group with heat applied to the mice in the box by means of thermal tapes so as to mimic the temperature changes taking place because of the heat of the healer's hands when he was holding the cages with the third group of mice.

A group receiving the laying on of hands treatment for twenty days.

Benefits were observed in the third group compared to the other two groups.

"Studies were conducted both in our lab and in the Department of Physiology of the University of Manitoba. The results of this experiment were published in the *International Journal of Parapsychology* and in the *Journal for the American Society of Psychical Research*," the scientist noted.

"In plants, we began our studies just as we did with mice," Dr. Grad said. The results were equally as good as with the animals.

Next they set up an experiment using ordinary people, not a verified holistic faith healer.

One was a person that Dr. Grad referred to as Mr. B., who had helped in the previous experiments. "Now, he has a passion for plants and is able to make them grow and thrive," Dr. Grad said.

"The other two people were depressive patients in the hospital where I worked. One of them had a psychotic depression and the other one had a neurotic depression. I had obtained permission from their doctors to give them each a bottle to hold, during which time the bottle was to be in a brown paper bag as part of the multi-blind system of the experiment. Each person was asked to hold the bottle for half an hour.

"When I came to the man who was more deeply depressed of the two, he didn't even ask me why I was giving him the bottle. I was wearing a white coat, as I usually do, and he thought I was a medical doctor coming to prepare him for electric shock therapy and he told me he didn't need any." The man agreed to hold the bag with the bottle in it.

"The other patient was a young woman. When I came to see her she had a neurotic depression. She was depressed, but less severely so than the man, and she was sitting somewhat forlornly in an outpatient department. When I came up to her and asked her if she would be kind enough to hold the bottle for half an hour, she was a little taken aback and asked, 'Well, why are you giving me this to hold?'

"I told her that this was part of an experiment; we wanted her to hold the bottle in her hand and later on we wanted to put the saline solution on some plants. She thought this was a great idea and she brightened right up and this upset me, because I didn't want her to become enthusiastic. In fact, I chose her for the experiment just for the opposite reasons. So there we were and the die was cast and I decided we would just go ahead with the experiment.

"When I came back half an hour later she was faithfully holding the bottle, somewhat like a mother holding a child, I thought, in a kind of cradling fashion. I didn't know what to make of all of this but I was going to see what would happen in any case.

"The group that grew the slowest was the one watered by saline held by the man with the psychotic depression.

"The next lowest group was the untreated control, the bottle not held by anybody.

"The next lowest group was that of the girl who had the neurotic depression.

"The best one was Mr. B.'s group.

"Now, I had supposed that this girl's plants would grow more slowly than the control, but this was not so, and I attribute this to the fact that she was quite enthusiastic about the experiment. The interesting thing is it is not the diagnosis which is important for this experiment; what is important is the state of mind you are in at the moment.

"There are quite a few implications arising from this study. Perhaps the most critical implication of all is the fact that it says that anybody handling any material imparts to that material something that bears a relation to his emotional state. I assume that some energy was at the core of this transfer, for it took place through the glass wall of the bottle containing the saline solution."

He went on to say that "this research could help to explain why some physicians are more effective than others (this has something to do with what we call the bedside manner) and why some nurses, for example, can have a profound effect on patients, depending on what their attitude is.

"Also, we know for example in psychotherapy, where a patient comes to a doctor repeatedly, that there is a kind of relationship that develops between psychiatrist and patient which Freud called transference. Now, I believe there is an energy process at work here, and I think that this process is at work between parents and children, teachers and students, man and wife, and in the old days between the pharmacist and the medication he prepared.

"Some children are very disturbed because there is a lack of we call it rapport. Rapport describes an energy process, I believe—something passing between parent and child which may be positive or the opposite."

As he reached the end of his presentation, Dr. Grad hinted that the transference of energy to objects—what we call psychometry—could have profound effects in everyday life:

"Then there is the relationship of a mother to cooking," he said. "She has a responsibility there, and I can expand further on this, but time does not allow. Thank you."

CHAPTER 6

Learn Advanced ESP in 10 Days or Less

You already have everything you need to unleash your own psychic ability. The only thing lacking is awareness.

It is like learning to read. Nothing can block you from learning if you want to learn, and you follow the simple instructions.

Expansion of consciousness is like discovering that you have two legs instead of just one. Imagine if 90 percent of people thought they could only use one leg at a time while you used both of yours.

We all have another set of senses besides our physical senses of sight, sound, touch, taste, and smell.

We have mental senses. Senses of the psyche. Psychic senses.

Some people seem to know how to say the right thing at the right time. Do they have a better understanding of human nature? In a way, yes—because they are using both sets of senses to observe what people are saying, doing, and thinking.

The Best Kind of ESP

Trained psychics have an advantage because they have a system that produces reliable and repeatable results.

This also applies to the naturally developed psychics we discussed in Chapter 1 when they take the Silva training and practice using it.

The best psychics—naturals or trained—average approximately 80 percent overall accuracy. That's excellent. If you can be right four out of five times, then people will consider you a genius.

Even better for trained psychics: they often know when they are not detecting accurate information, so they don't give you wrong answers.

Is there a way that trained psychics can be accurate 100 percent of the time? Yes, by working together with other similarly trained psychics and using the "Correlation Method" that you can learn in Chapter 31. They can coordinate their psychic information with other trained psychics who use the same system they use.

Activating the Dormant Part of Your Brain

Developing your ESP is easy because all you need to do is follow simple instructions and learn to use the psychic part of your brain.

You learned in Chapter 1 that we all have two sets of sensing faculties for detecting information about people, places, things, and events:

Information detected with your objective—physical—senses is impressed on the left brain hemisphere, and a copy is transferred to the right brain hemisphere.

Information detected with your subjective—psychic—senses is impressed on your right brain hemisphere. But for most people it is not transferred to their left hemisphere.

Therefore, most people—90 percent—only have conscious access to information they detected with their physical senses.

Their right brain hemisphere has twice as much information as the left, but 90 percent of people don't know how to access it or retrieve it.

It is like a person with two good legs but who only uses one leg. If they start using both legs they will do much more than double their ability to walk and run and dance.

To help understand why 90 percent of people are growing up without learning to use their ESP the way the other 10 percent do, we need to know how the brain works.

How Your Brain Works

"It takes the child about seven years to mature the brain," José Silva explained. "So for seven years, the mind of the human being is functioning inductively, which means there's no human intelligence. In other words, their mind cannot improve anything. It can function in the environment perfectly well, but cannot improve anything."

Around the age of seven the child's mind changes from inductive functioning to deductive functioning. The child can now analyze information and solve problems.

The next stage of brain development comes at approximately 14 years old.

The alpha brain wave frequencies from 7 to 14 cycles per second (cps) are ideal for thinking.

The higher beta frequencies, from 14 to 21 cps, are for taking action.

José Silva realized why most people don't develop psychic ability:

"A child, while learning between 7 and 14 years of age, continues to learn by seeing first, concentrating on focusing," he said. "We think that's the sense that throws us off from developing correctly, because you got stuck on using mostly the beta instead of the alpha.

"So we forgot the alpha and it became dormant and beta became the strongest sense to focus on.

"We should have developed alpha first before the beta," he continued. "Alpha became dormant and beta became very active. This is where the problem started, developing the wrong part of the brain, the left brain."

The Silva ESP training corrects that by first helping you learn to use the alpha brainwave region with conscious awareness.

"We found the proper training, proper exercises to slow down the brain frequency so the mind can then use those lower brain frequencies. Mind can then become attuned to alpha and operate from alpha and become aware or conscious of the information in the subconscious," Silva noted.

In other words, using the subconscious consciously. The subconscious then becomes an "inner conscious level."

Once you are at the alpha level, with your eyes closed, you use visualization and imagination to detect information that is already impressed on your brain neurons, and to add new information you detect with your psychic senses.

Then as you practice using your subjective sensing faculties to detect information and solve problems, you start using your

ESP just as naturally as you use your physical senses to see, hear, touch, taste, and smell.

The First Clue Emerges

During one of their study sessions, José Silva was surprised when his 10-year-old daughter answered him before he had asked his question.

It had been a routine study session up to that point:

He had prepared a list of poems he had read to her in a previous session. The list was not in the same order he had read them to her. He changed the order to make it more difficult for her.

Then he hypnotized her as he had been doing for a couple of years, and she said, "The first one you want is...," and she recited it. Then she recited the next one. And the next one.

"It was as though she was guessing my mind," he recalled.

Instead of getting back on track with teaching her the schoolwork, he devised some new tests to see if she really was "guessing my mind."

He asked her about some things he didn't know. For instance, he gave her a street address and asked her what was there, and she told him. When they drove to that address and looked, she had described the building perfectly, even telling him how many rows of bricks there were.

Learning from Those Who Came Before

How did this happen? Was it something to do with hypnosis? Then he recalled something he had heard when he was stationed in Bowling Green, Kentucky, when he was in the Army in

1946. It was about a psychic named Edgar Cayce, "The Sleeping Prophet."

He recalled that Cayce developed his psychic abilities after a hypnotist helped him overcome a serious health problem.

Isabel's psychic ability emerged after she had gone through many hypnotic sessions to help her learn her schoolwork.

In 1953 the ten-year-old child started doing something that hypnotized subjects don't do: asking questions and taking control of the session.

He realized that she was in a state of mind comparable to light sleep, but she still had conscious awareness.

Just like "The Sleeping Prophet."

It wasn't hypnosis and it wasn't sleep—so what was it? It was something new. She was using the subconsciously consciously. But that's a contradiction in terms, so he named it the "inner conscious level."

More importantly, he wanted to know how he could induce that state of consciousness in other people.

Very simple: Play a little trick on the brain. Make the brain think you are ready to go to sleep, and the brain will slow down.

What do most people do when they are ready to go to sleep?

- You find a comfortable position
- Close your eyes
- Relax your body
- Relax mentally

Sound familiar? That is how we guide you to find the alpha brainwave level.

So why don't people go straight to sleep when we read the Centering Exercise to them?

Because we give you something to do—not enough to bring you back to beta, but enough to keep you from going to lower brain frequencies:

We instruct you to visualize some tranquil and passive scenes, to mentally repeat some beneficial statements, to project yourself mentally to your ideal place of relaxation, and so on.

José Silva explained it this way:

"You used to have just two states of consciousness: Awake and asleep.

"Now you are creating a third state of consciousness by learning to use the subconscious consciously.

"That's why it is important for students to maintain awareness throughout the conditioning cycle. We would rather you be on the edge of beta rather than lose conscious awareness during the conditioning cycles."

Reactivating the Dormant Part of the Brain

How did he help the children develop their ESP?

Once his young subjects were at that in-between level that scientists were calling the alpha level, he asked them to recall their previous experiences with various items: what each item looked like, felt like, its taste and smell and sound. He reasoned that this would help them to recognize these items when they detected them later with their mind.

Here is his explanation:

"When you are at your level and visualizing and imagining (thinking about what things look like), you are impressing those experiences on both your left and your right brain hemispheres. This happens because when you are at your level, at the alpha level, there is a connection with the right brain hemisphere. You are synchronizing the two brain hemispheres.

"The first thing you do in the ESP training is to recall experiences already stored on your left brain hemisphere.

"You recall these stored experiences at your level, and you transfer them to your right brain hemisphere. Then the next thing you do is use your imagination to sense information with your subjective senses, with your right brain hemisphere, and you store these new experiences on both brain hemispheres.

"In the ESP training, when you project into your living room wall, into the metals, into the leaves and to the pet, you are storing experiences on your right brain hemisphere.

"When you study human anatomy from a psychic point of view, you do the same thing. You recall a relative or friend and, while at your level, transfer these memories—this stored information—to your right brain hemisphere.

"Then you sense information subjectively and store this on both brain hemispheres.

"Now you have points of reference on your right brain hemisphere that you will use when working health cases of people you do not know," he said.

"In the beginning, if you desire to use your right brain hemisphere, you must enter your level and call on the experiences you have already stored on your right brain hemisphere as you went through the Silva ESP training.

"But as you store more and more experiences on your right brain hemisphere, an interesting phenomenon takes place:

"You begin to develop the ability to use both brain hemispheres without closing your eyes (provided your vision is defocused) and without having to use the standard 3 to 1 method to enter your level.

"Your brain automatically dips into alpha approximately 30 times every minute. This is true for all people, whether they are Silva graduates or not.

"The brain stays at alpha for only a very short period of time, but this time can be very useful if you have points of reference to work with on the right brain hemisphere.

"With practice, you can learn to make those brief trips to alpha last longer.

"If you have not stored any experiences on your right brain hemisphere, which you do by visualizing and imagining while at the alpha level, then you will be unable to do any right brain thinking during these brief trips to alpha, because you do not have any points of reference to guide you.

"But after you have stored experiences with your right brain hemisphere, you can then begin to develop the ability to use your right brain hemisphere for thinking when your brain dips into alpha for those fractions of a second.

"You can sense information with your subjective senses when your brain dips into alpha, but only if you have points of reference (experiences) on your right brain hemisphere to guide you, and you learn to recognize that special feeling of being at alpha and stay longer than that brief instant.

"You can program for things you desire with your right brain hemisphere when your brain dips into alpha, but only if you have points of reference (experiences) on your right brain hemisphere to guide you, and you learn to recognize that special feeling of being at alpha and stay longer than that brief instant.

"That is why it is important to practice all of the Silva techniques, especially caseworking. You want to store as many experiences as possible using your right brain hemisphere, not only visualizing and imagining, but sensing information and programming for your desired end results.

"Now we are back to where we started: visualization and imagination.

"When you practice thinking about what things look like while you are at your level and are using your right brain hemisphere, you are doing exactly what is necessary to bring about the results you desire.

"A person who is not a Silva graduate can practice visualizing and imagining all day long, can have extremely clear imagery, but still get very poor results if they are using only the left brain hemisphere and they do not know how to enter the alpha level and make points of reference on the right brain hemisphere.

"A Silva graduate who practices going to level and thinking about what things look like, who practices the techniques, and practices caseworking, will develop the ability to achieve any goals because the Silva graduate is using both brain hemispheres."

There are complete instructions for doing this in Part 3 of this Master Course.

CHAPTER 7

Spiritual ESP: Help Line to the Other Side

How valuable would it be to have a personal tutor who knows what lies ahead for you, who knows what people are planning, and could guide you to be better prepared to avoid danger and to take advantages of opportunities?

Would you like a real-life example? Who better than José Silva, born poor, orphaned at age four, never went to school a day in his life as a student because he had to shine shoes and do odd jobs for money to help support the family, yet look at all he achieved:

Learned radio repair in a correspondence course when he was 14, and that eventually made him a millionaire.

His curiosity led him to the study of psychology and his groundbreaking research into the mind and human potential.

Patented several electronic devices that he invented, including one that states that human concentration turns on an educational program.

You wouldn't be reading this book today, we wouldn't have the Silva courses today, and we wouldn't have the MentalVideo Technique if higher intelligence hadn't encouraged him, guided him, and admonished him.

Here is one experience he wrote about in his autobiography.

A Special Visitor Comes into My Home
by José Silva

It was in 1953 that I tested my first trained subject and then wrote to Dr. J. B. Rhine about it. Dr. Rhine was head of the parapsychology department at Duke University in Durham, North Carolina, and a leader in testing people who had this PSI factor.

Dr. Rhine was adamant in saying that the psi factor was like the IQ factor, that some people had more and some had less, and that neither the psi nor the IQ factor could be enhanced.

The way I saw it, both could be enhanced.

The IQ factor is merely a measurement of how many problems you can solve on a test in a certain period of time. I started helping children to do better in school.

When a child uses more brain energy to impress information on brain cells, the child has better recall and better memory. The more information that a person recalls, the more problems that person will be able to solve.

That's how I believe intelligence should be measured: by the person's problem-solving capacity. The more problems a person is able to solve, the more successful the person is bound to be in everything.

Dr. Rhine told me that clairvoyants (people with good guessing ability, with an enhanced psi factor) were born, not taught, and that my big mistake was not having pre-tested my subject. Dr. Rhine hinted that I, not knowing any better, was working with a natural clairvoyant to begin with.

I did not know that to prove things to an academic scientist I had to pre-test a subject to see how much of the PSI factor the subject had to begin with. I figured that the number one man in parapsychology was saying it, so it must be right.

Besides, what Dr. Rhine said to me made a lot of sense, but the thought of starting all over again was just too much for me. It had taken three years to get where I was, and that turned out to be a big "Zero" according to Dr. Rhine.

It was with these bleak thoughts on a dismal, cloudy Saturday morning that I decided to quit this nonsense.

I thought about my previous experiences, how I started to study psychology after meeting the psychiatrist, about the picture of Christ in my wallet, the light in the night five years later and the Christ awareness and the lottery ticket that won me $10,000.

As I finished packing my psychology books and storing them in the attic, it started to rain. It really poured, with thunder, lightning, the whole works.

As the rain calmed down a little, the children went out to play in the rain. The water was flowing down our unpaved street like a muddy river. I sat in the house, on the same couch under which the psychology book had ended up when I threw it across the room and resolved not to waste my time anymore on things that didn't make any sense to me.

My mind reached back into the memories, the feelings associated with the research I had done to that point, the research that now had come to a dead end.

I remembered reading a poem about "One Solitary Life" at the Army reception center with tears in my eyes.

I recalled the dreamlike experience with the numbers that are burned into my memory forever, along with the Christ awareness, and the lottery ticket my friend found late the next night.

Did that get me back to studying psychology? I wondered. *Where does Christ come in and why?*

Suddenly Ricardo, my second son, who was almost ten years old, came bursting through the front door and interrupted my thoughts.

It was still drizzling outside, and Ricardo was dripping water on the floor as he came running toward me.

"I found this outside," he exclaimed as he dropped a roll of heavy paper on the table, then turned and ran back outside, leaving his treasure behind.

As my gaze locked onto the heavy roll of paper, something attracted my attention immediately:

The roll of paper appeared to be dry!

I picked it up and sure enough, it was dry.

When I unrolled it, I got the surprise of my life, a shock that brought me to my knees again.

Christ was staring at me.

It was a large picture of Christ, just His head and shoulders, but as large as life, looking at me with dark, piercing eyes, not judging, but full of love and compassion, and I felt as though He was asking:

"Why did you stop studying? Did I not tell you to study psychology?"

Tears came to my eyes, and I felt as though I had been a bad boy for not obeying.

I went into the bathroom and had a good cry, swearing that I would continue with this work, and not ever again stop for the rest of my life, even if it meant giving up my very successful electronics business.

I went into the bathroom because I did not want Paula or the children to see me crying. It would have been very difficult for a man almost 40 years old to explain the reason. I had not cried like this since my grandmother, who had raised me, passed away.

Once again, I got out my psychology books.

I framed the large picture of Christ, and it has been hanging in my office ever since.

This last experience, with the picture of Christ, gave me more determination than ever before.

I also consider this experience to be responsible for my system, developed through research, being brought to millions of people throughout the world, helping them become more spiritual, more healthy, wealthy, successful, and happy human beings.

I named the picture of Christ "The Ecumenical Christ" and started to study the Bible more seriously. I was trying to find a connection between Christ and my study of psychology.

Two Programming Technique
by Ed Bernd Jr.

There are two formula-type techniques you can use to help you solve problems and create successful outcomes.

Before you resort to asking higher intelligence for help, it is essential that you try to solve the problem yourself. That is why we were sent here to planet Earth. The 3-Scenes Technique helps you with that:

The 3-Scenes Technique

When you desire to use the 3-Scenes Technique, go to your center with the 3 to 1 method. Create and project onto your Mental Screen, directly in front of you, using visualization, an image of the existing situation.

Recall details of what the situation looks like in this first scene. Make a good study of the existing situation so you are completely aware of all aspects of it.

If you programmed for this project previously, then take into account any changes that have taken place since your most recent programming session.

After making a good study of the existing situation, shift your awareness to your left, approximately 15 degrees. In a second scene, to the left of the first scene, use imagination to mentally picture yourself taking action and doing something to implement your decisions, and to follow the guidance you have received, and imagine the desired changes beginning to take place.

Now in a third scene, another 15 degrees farther to your left, use your imagination to create and project an image of the situation the way you desire for it to end up. Imagine many people benefiting. The more people who benefit, the better.

Anytime in the future when you think of this project, visualize (recall) the image that you created of the desired end result in the third scene.

If your efforts aren't producing results, then you can ask higher intelligence to help or to send you an indication of how to proceed.

Remember that higher intelligence wants to improve living conditions on the planet, so review the Laws of Programming and make sure you are in compliance. We discuss them in the next chapter.

The MentalVideo Technique

Programming a technique, the MentalVideo Technique, that you can use for problem-solving.

Whenever you need to solve a problem, make a decision, or obtain guidance with the MentalVideo Technique, proceed in the following manner:

At beta, with your eyes open, mentally create, with visualization, a MentalVideo of a problem, or the existing situation. Include everything that belongs to the animate matter kingdom. Animate matter means everything that contains life.

After you have completed the MentalVideo of the problem, use visualization to review it at beta, with your eyes closed.

Later, when you are in bed and ready to go to sleep, go to your center with the 3 to 1 method. Once you are at your center, review the MentalVideo that you created of the problem, or the existing situation, when you were at the beta level.

After you have reviewed the problem, mentally convert the problem into a project. Then create, with imagination, a MentalVideo of the solution.

The MentalVideo of the solution should contain a step-by-step procedure of how you desire the project to be resolved.

After both of the MentalVideos have been completed, go to sleep with the intention of delivering the MentalVideos to your tutor while you sleep. Take for granted that the delivery will be made.

During the next three days, look for indications that point to the solution. Every time you think of the project, think of the solution that you created in the MentalVideo, in a past tense sense.

Who Is Your Tutor?

Your tutor is part of the management team that governs the universe.

José Silva said it didn't make sense that one entity that was powerful enough and intelligent enough to create the whole universe would want to govern all of it without any help. It made sense to him that this entity would have a management team, just like there are many people at various levels of city and state and national government who help to keep things running smoothly.

Perhaps our management structures in government, business, the military, sports leagues, and many other places are based on the management structure of the universe.

Religions suggest that when they talk about angels and archangels and such.

José Silva wanted a non-religious term for our contact with the next level above us so he chose the term "tutor." He defined the tutor this way:

"The Universe has billions of galaxies. Our galaxy, which is considered a baby galaxy compared to others, has millions of solar systems. In order to oversee the whole universe it is necessary to have a hierarchy of God.

"Common sense indicates that God must have billions of helpers. Some call these helpers angels, archangels, and seraphs; others call them guides, etc.

"Everyone has a personal representative; we refer to your representative as your tutor.

"The tutor is the spiritual guide that resides in the spiritual, subjective dimension (the other side) and is connected to the hierarchy of God to help you solve problems when you are doing the right thing. Your tutor serves as your personal God."

You Are Special Too

We are all part of this management system. Indications are that we were sent here to planet Earth with a job to do. That job is to correct problems, improve living conditions, and convert the planet into a paragraph.

In order to do our job, we have been given dominion over the planet. We are the highest biological life form on the planet; we have been assigned a superior position and have been given dominion over the planet.

That makes you and everybody else on planet Earth part of the management team that we refer to as higher intelligence.

"We are gods on the planet," José Silva said. "Anything that God can do in the universe, we can do on planet Earth."

The Mental Screen

Some people find it easier to detect and imagine what things look like if they have a "Mental Screen" to project mental images onto.

To locate your Mental Screen, begin with your eyes closed, turned slightly upward from the horizontal plane of sight, at an angle of approximately 20 degrees. The area that you perceive with your mind is your Mental Screen.

Without using your eyelids as screens, sense your Mental Screen to be out, away from your body. To improve the use of your Mental Screen, project images or mental pictures onto the screen, especially images having color. Concentrate on mentally sensing and visualizing true color.

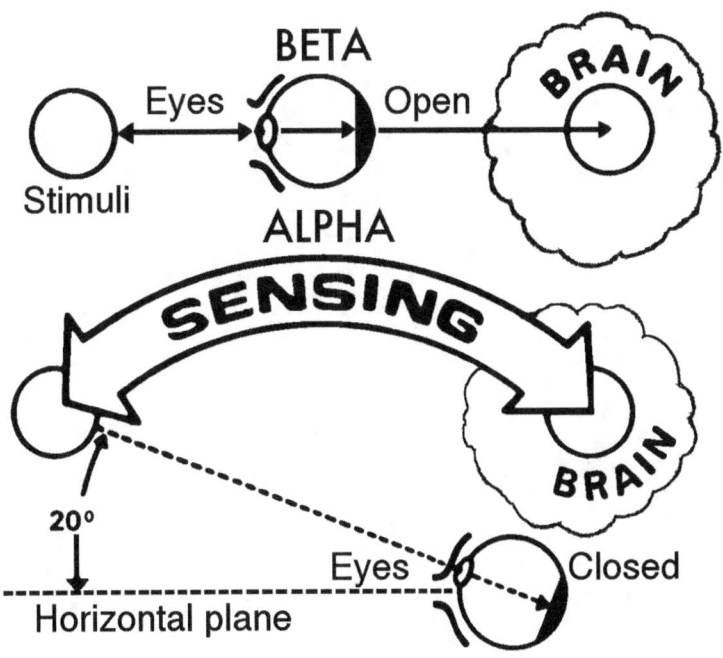

Part 2
Keys to the Kingdom Within

CHAPTER 8

The Secret to a Prosperous and Meaningful Life

"The World Was Not Made for Just One Person"
—JOSÉ SILVA

There are several motivational strategies and techniques embedded in José Silva's courses to help you achieve more successes and to achieve them faster.

The first Beneficial Statement in the course is a good example:

"My increasing mental faculties are for serving humanity better."

Some people question that, saying, "I need to take care of myself first." Others point out the benefits. Both make some good points.

An author named Bob Berg has written a series of bestselling books about being a Go-Giver. He explains that most people don't give you money because you want it. They give you money because you do something of value to them.

Learn What People Want and Help Them Get It

José Silva figured that out when he was six years old. His father had been killed a couple of years earlier, and his mother had remarried and moved away. As the eldest male in the family, he felt he had a responsibility to help provide for them.

Some children in the community might beg or steal, but he thought there was a better way: Give people something they wanted and they would pay him for it. So he started shining shoes. Then when he saw people looking at big sheets of paper, he made inquiries and started providing a newspaper to his shoeshine customers, and they paid him for the added service.

When he heard two men talking about needing somebody reliable to clean their offices at night, he spoke up, and they gave him an opportunity to show what he could do. While cleaning the offices he found a watch and some cash and put them in a drawer, out of sight. The next day he came to the office and told them what he had found.

They had been testing him, of course, and when they saw that he cared as much about them as he cared about himself, they told him the cleaning job was his for as long as he wanted it.

Expanding That Idea

Within a few years he was hiring and training other youngsters for a new business venture.

The 14-year-old entrepreneur would travel to San Antonio, about three hours north of Laredo, and buy household staples: cleaning products, sewing supplies, cooking utensils. He would bring them back to Laredo and have his young partners go door-to-door selling them, and then split the profit equally with them.

How much were they earning? The typical adult worker in Laredo at the time was earning about a dollar a week.

Young José's partners were earning a dollar a day, and José was earning 10 dollars a day. That was enough money that he didn't have to think twice when a new opportunity came along in the form of a correspondence course in a new field: radio repair.

He had gone to a barbershop to practice his reading. He had never attended school as a student so he had to learn to read and write on his own. He had been reading comic books because the pictures helped him understand what the characters were saying.

He asked the barber if he could borrow the correspondence course.

The barber replied that it was a very valuable course, and he would rent it to him for a dollar a lesson, provided that he fill out the lessons in the barber's name. He quickly agreed.

Both of them got something they wanted:

The barber made a profit by renting the course, and he got a nice diploma that he hung on his barbershop wall for everyone to see.

José Silva got an education that helped make him a millionaire, and also helped him understand aspects of the human brain that many scientists still don't fully understand.

Even at 14 years old, José Silva had earned a reputation for honesty and doing whatever he promised to do, so the owner of a local electronics store took a fatherly interest in him. He would give the youngster whatever parts he needed and let him pay after the customer paid him for the repairs.

A half century later the owner of the store needed help and José Silva was able to help.

"We are Fingers on the Hands of God"

The last paragraph in the UltraMind ESP System conditioning cycles includes a statement that provides motivation and guidance to help us understand why that is a valuable way to approach life:

"You will continue to strive to take part in constructive and creative activities to make this a better world to live in, so that when we move on, we shall have left behind a better world for those who follow. You will consider the whole of humanity, depending on their ages, as fathers or mothers, brothers or sisters, sons or daughters. You are a superior human being; you have greater understanding, compassion, and patience with others."

I was presenting the Silva ESP training here in Laredo one weekend when I suddenly realized how profound an idea it is to consider everybody, depending on their ages, "as fathers or mothers, brothers or sisters, sons or daughters." On Monday I asked Mr. Silva about it:

"That's a statement of unselfishness, isn't it?"

He stared at me for a moment with an expression that was a mixture of surprise, respect, and gratitude, and replied:

"If it weren't for that attitude, we wouldn't have the Silva Method today."

Other People with the Same Idea

Albert Einstein said that we are all part of a whole that we call the universe and we should embrace all living things.

Biologist Bruce Lipton wrote in his book *The Biology of Belief* that humans must learn to work together or humanity will wind up like a diseased organ, with cells malfunctioning and not contributing to the well-being of the organism.

To paraphrase the late civil rights leader Martin Luther King Jr., we are all woven into the fabric of humanity, and anything that affects one of us directly affects the rest of us indirectly.

Robert B. Stone, author and coauthor of several Silva books, reminded us that we must remember our bigger responsibilities. He said that we all come from the same Creative Source. "Scientists recognize the oneness but they have different words for it," he said.

"Non-local mind is a way of saying exactly the same thing. Carl Jung, one of the founders of psychology, called it the collective unconscious. British biologist Rupert Sheldrake calls it the morphogenetic field. Religionists, on the other hand, call it God."

José Silva had a simple way of explaining this idea: "We are fingers on the hands of God." We have physical bodies so we can do the physical work as higher intelligence directs.

We must not ignore our own needs of course.

Giuseppe Lonero, a Silva student from Sicily, explained it this way: "Sometimes, when I hit my pinky toe on a corner, I forget about the beauty of nature for a couple of seconds, or a bit more."

In Florida we say that "when we are up to our waist in alligators it can be hard to remember that our main job is to drain the swamp." Sometimes we have to put our immediate needs first.

José Silva's brother Juan explained that when doing business, "José never wanted to get the best of somebody else, and he darn sure didn't want them to get the best of him."

The Laws of Programming

To help us live a meaningful life and help ourselves and others, José Silva developed the Laws of Programming and included them in the UltraMind ESP System.

The following laws are to be considered when programming:

- You should do to others only what you like others to do to you.
- The solution must help to make this planet a better place to live.
- It must be the best for everybody concerned.
- It must help at least two or more persons.
- It must be within the possibility area.

If there weren't a lot of people who want their life to be meaningful and provide help and support for our universal family, then the old 1946 movie *It's A Wonderful Life* wouldn't still be one of the most popular holiday movies every year.

If we are a part of the human family on planet Earth, then isn't the smart thing to help—not hurt—our family?

When humanity does well, we all do well. A rising tide lifts all ships.

CHAPTER 9

The State of Scientific Investigation of ESP

Now you know more about ESP than most scientists.

Why?

Because you are investigating it and they are not.

Now we know the sun and moon and stars don't rotate around the Earth, that the Earth isn't flat, that heavier objects don't fall to Earth faster than lighter ones.

Perhaps the next giant leap forward for traditional science will be the realization that there is something more than the physical world. There is a world that cannot be detected directly by physical instruments or biological sensing faculties but is able to affect our physical bodies and the world we live in.

For those who deny that, we have a simple question: How much do you love your spouse, your children?

Do you have a physical instrument that can detect how much love you have for them? You can measure the effect your love has on your body and on them, but "love" is not a tangible, physical substance like flesh and blood. It is impossible to touch "love," to describe it exactly, to bottle it, or to give an exact value.

The mind is the same. It is not tangible, but the effect it has on the physical world is very real even if it cannot be touched, measured, or described.

The Built-in Bias of Traditional Science

Scientists have strict rules to prevent bias in their scientific investigations, which is ironic because their bias in accepting only objective—physical world—explanations is what prevents them from discovering a whole new dimension.

José Silva was not constrained by that kind of thinking. He simply investigated whatever was in front of him and discovered how to expand consciousness in many ways.

He developed a simple procedure to expand our consciousness into what psychologists were calling the "subconscious" so we can "use the subconscious consciously." Since it is no longer sub—or beneath—our conscious awareness, we now call it the "inner conscious level."

When his ten-year-old daughter began "guessing his mind," he didn't dismiss it as "coincidence." He investigated it. His daughter's psychic accuracy was far beyond chance level, so he kept investigating and found a simple way for everybody to develop their ESP and expand their conscious awareness beyond the limitations of our five physical senses. You can learn this system in Part 3 of this book.

His ultimate consciousness expansion achievement came less than two years before his passing: a scientifically based way to obtain guidance and help from higher intelligence on "the other side."

"Higher intelligence" refers to what some people call God or Jehovah or Allah or The Almighty or Brahman or Yahweh or many other names.

"The other side" is the dimension that we come from when we are born and return to when we die. It is also known as Heaven, Nirvana, Paradise, Jinnah, and other terms.

Chasing Conformity

There is a huge amount of pressure on research scientists to conform to proven theories rather than try to break completely new ground. This pressure begins when they are in college and their professors demand that they cite accepted research when they present their own ideas.

It is okay to expand on what is already known, but not to introduce new knowledge into the "scientific community."

Scientists are validated by having their research published in a peer-reviewed scientific journal.

In that way science and religion are a lot alike: both require their followers to adhere to their rigid doctrines. Both have very exclusive doctrines: traditional science considers physics to be the basis of everything while religions predict dire consequences for those who don't believe in the spiritual origins of everything.

Both have well-developed arguments for their position, yet the whole truth lies in a blending of the two concepts. Attempting to expand their consciousness can have serious consequences.

In the early seventeenth century, Galileo Galilei confirmed what astronomer Nicolaus Copernicus had found a century earlier: that the Earth revolves around the sun, not the other way around. But the church started an inquisition process against him and forced him to say it was only theory.

Dare to Be Transformative

Where is the new generation of courageous researchers who will march with us into this new frontier?

Those who are remembered, whose work is taught to future generations of scientists, are those who have the courage to go where others fear to tread.

Even Einstein failed, but failure didn't deter him.

Somebody will get the credit for future discoveries in the field of metaphysics. And discoveries *will* come; they cannot be stopped. Just like the establishment couldn't stop Copernicus, Galileo, and Bruno when they proclaimed that the Earth is not the center of everything, that the sun doesn't revolve around the Earth.

Some Courageous Explorers

While some scientists choose to believe an illusionist—a former stage magician whose job is to deceive people—others dare to break free of the constraints of conformity and learn what is really going on in this new field of psychorientology (psych-orient-ology—the study of how to direct and use your mind for greater success).

Anybody can be a critic. But there is nothing "amazing" about using your talent to deceive to dissuade curious scientists from conducting research that could lead to beneficial breakthroughs that help humanity.

Here are some examples of researchers who have actually done amazing work that people are benefiting from.

Cleve Backster connected his polygraph (lie detector) to a dragon tree one night and discovered a primary means of communication that we all have whether we know it or not.

All he did was think about burning one of the leaves and a dramatic response was produced on the polygraph.

"There was no doubt in my mind," he said, "that the plant was aware of my thought." He spent the remaining thirty-six years of his life studying this "primary perception" phenomenon.

Backster's research also revealed that we communicate with our own body cells even when they are several miles away.

His research also demonstrates repeatedly that the attitude of the researcher affects the results. But try explaining that to a conventional scientist.

One researcher who decided to duplicate Backster's first experience with the dragon tree said that there was no response from the plant.

Backster asked if he intended to actually burn the plant.

The scientist said, "No, you didn't burn the plant, so I didn't plan to burn it."

"But I *intended* to burn it," Backster replied. "There is a difference between *pretend* and *intend*."

In other words, if the plant can become aware of your thoughts about harming it, it can also sense that you don't actually intend to harm it. That seems obvious, doesn't it?

You can read about Backster's research in the book *The Secret Life of Your Cells* by prolific Silva author Robert B. Stone.

The book includes a chapter about the significance of this work to José Silva's research.

Wilder Penfield was a highly respected Canadian neurosurgeon in the mid-twentieth century. While José Silva was developing his Silva Mind Control course, Dr. Penfield was writing that the mind is a function of the brain.

But after decades of work in the field, he concluded that the mind cannot be explained solely as a function of the brain. He had the courage to report on his new belief that mind possesses non-physical attributes that cannot be ascribed to brain activity. He wrote about this in his 1975 book *The Mystery of the Mind*.

While some researchers conducted their own investigations to see if they could confirm Penfield's experiences, others chose to criticize and find reasons to dismiss his findings.

That reminds me of what former United States President Theodore Roosevelt said, that it is not the critic who counts. The credit belongs to the one who is actually in the arena, who at the best knows in the end the triumph of high achievement, and who at the worst, if he fails, at least fails while daring greatly, so that his place shall never be with those cold and timid souls who know neither victory nor defeat.

Biologist Bruce Lipton is another scientist who had the courage to publish his findings that parallel what José Silva discovered in his research.

Lipton acknowledges in his book *The Biology of Belief,* first published in 2005, that consciousness is something separate from physics, something that isn't limited by space and time, something that pushes us to work together in harmony for the common good. If we don't, he said, "humanity will wind up like a diseased organ, with cells malfunctioning and not contributing to the well-being of the organism."

John Mihalasky headed up a ten-year research project at Newark College of Engineering (now New Jersey Technical Institute) in the 1960s and found that the most successful business executives have the most ESP.

In experiments he performed with company CEOs, he observed that the CEOs with the best success rates at running their business (measured in terms of five-year profitability growth) performed best in tests of precognitive ability.

His research also revealed factors that can help or hinder your ability to use ESP. We included many more details in our book *Silva UltraMind Systems ESP for Business Success* published by G&D Media in 2019.

Detecting the Mind and Consciousness

How can something exist if it is not physical?

We cannot explain it either, except to say that mind and consciousness are not physical but nevertheless exist in the universe. Since they are not physical, there are no physical instruments or physical senses that can detect them.

But we can detect the effects and can see what they do.

It is a little like a night in 1962 when I was riding on midnight patrol with a police officer. He was driving down a street in an industrial area and shining his spotlight at buildings along the way, looking for broken windows that might indicate a break-in.

"You must have really good eyesight to see broken glass at this distance," I said.

"I am not looking for broken glass," he replied. "I am looking for the reflection of the spotlight in the windows. If the light is not reflected back to me, then I know something is wrong."

That concept served me well throughout my newspaper career and beyond. If I didn't understand what was going on, I looked for somebody who did.

Like the time an LP gas truck caught fire in the middle of Atlanta. I was eighteen years old and interning on the award-winning photo staff of the *Atlanta Journal-Constitution*.

There were fire trucks everywhere and dozens of firefighters, so I just looked for the fire chief—he was the only person who had a different color hat than everyone else.

When I spotted him, I got behind him and pointed my camera at what he was looking at and took a picture that the *Atlanta Journal* ran on the front page that afternoon. Not bad for an 18-year-old intern. In fact, they offered me a permanent job at the end of the summer. And all I had done was locate the person who knew what was happening.

But for some reason traditional scientists don't consider that a valid approach for scientific investigation.

Or they want to avoid being criticized and ostracized.

Science can only study the natural world. There is no accepted scientific mechanism to explain ESP, so only a few dare to even study it.

They also need to accept the idea that one person's mind can influence another person's mind, especially when the people are within range of the physical part of the human aura. Having disbelievers in the room can spoil a project.

Skepticism is fine. We tell students in our seminars, "We welcome skeptics, because a skeptic is someone who has 'an attitude of doubt,' according to Webster but is willing to give us a fair chance to prove our case.

"It is those who are closed-minded and won't give us a chance who get no benefit."

Scientists haven't "found" the mind, so they conclude that it doesn't exist. With that attitude they will never understand what it is. Too bad, for them, because the mind doesn't exist . . . in physics.

It doesn't exist in a "parallel universe," because that would be physical. Nor a dimension with "no time or space" because if there's no time or space there's no place for it to be, and no time to constrain it.

As recently as 600 years ago, scientists thought the Earth was flat and the sun and moon and stars evolved around it. Religions even tortured and killed people who suggested otherwise.

Then one day a sailor named Christopher Columbus dared to sail west, and when he didn't sail off the edge he showed that the Earth is round and somehow we stick to it.

Reality is what it is, whether establishment scientists, religions, and political leaders believe it or not.

As long as researchers continue to argue that there is no scientific evidence or logical basis for ESP, and restrain their investigations with the limitations of physics, they greatly diminish their opportunities to discover new theories that will lead them to the next great breakthrough into a new era.

So we need more courageous scientists to join us in the arena, to stop chasing publication and promotions and tenure, scientists who will expand on the existing research and let people know that the key to success, and perhaps to the salvation of humanity itself, is within the human mind.

The researchers who dare to ask the questions that they are being punished for asking are the ones who will be remembered by history for taking the next great leap in our understanding of ourselves and the world we live in.

One such scientist was way ahead of his time: Phineas Parkhurst Quimby. Now here is José Silva to tell us how Quimby influenced his research and helped him to understand the mind and psychic ability.

Phineas Parkhurst Quimby

by José Silva

Reprinted from his self-published book *Reflections*.

The person who impressed me the most as a researcher in the field of the mind was not one of the best known so-called greats, but he was one that if compared to the others would perhaps be lost. The name of the researcher I have in mind was Phineas Parkhurst Quimby, who was born in the year 1802 and who made his transition in the year 1866. Here was a man who became attuned to the same message of passing on to humanity Christ's discovery that human beings can and should function on more than one plane (the use of both hemispheres) with full awareness.

Dr. Quimby appears to have gone through everything we have experienced in our research with only minor differences. These minor differences from another point of view do make a great difference. For example, the coincidence of Quimby finding a naturally developed subject such as Lucius Burkmar. Observing what Lucius could do with his mind must have been the most important stimulating factor that caused Quimby to continue with his research.

There is quite a difference between using a subject who has a naturally developed faculty of clairvoyance (one who is using both brain hemispheres) and using a subject whose faculty of clairvoyance we had to develop by learning to use the right brain hemisphere. It took us nine years to develop the first, what we called "trained clairvoyant."

It appears that Quimby's objective was to become a healer using Lucius for the detection of problems in patients and for recommending a medication. It also appears that later Quimby himself, in an unknown way, became a clairvoyant and healed people with what he called "the silent method." It is apparent that Quimby valued very highly the faculty of clairvoyance in Lucius.

We believe that it is one thing to apply healing on a person whose health problem you become aware of beforehand through the use of the physical senses, and another thing to apply healing on a person whose health problem you become aware of through the use of the psychic senses or, in other words, through clairvoyance. We believe that the best thing is to detect the problem clairvoyantly, and to use that same level as the ideal level from which to apply psychic healing through clairvoyance.

Quimby found that Lucius could do with his mind what we have found highly developed clairvoyants able to do with their minds. Quimby then brought to our attention the value of clairvoyance. Now if clairvoyance is so valuable, how much value can we assign to the method that the Jewish Rabbi called Christ discovered on how to train or develop clairvoyants? The method he used when he said, "Behold therefore, I send you prophets and wisemen."

Considering the objectives of the Silva Method, the Silva Method is more like Christ's than it is like Quimby's. The Silva Method trains and develops clairvoyants to function like Lucius and like Quimby so that people can use their clairvoyance to become healthier, more intuitive and productive, and more successful problem-solving agents on this planet.

In the Silva Method we consider the real reality and the truthful truth to be only that which, when applied, solves problems for humanity.

The Silva Method confirms that Quimby was right on his discovery of a scientific method of what we now call scientific prayer healing. The healer using this method of prayer healing usually does better when the healer is told what the health problem is beforehand.

We believe that the Silva Method is going to do much more toward helping humanity in a one-hundred-year period. One reason for this is a comparison of how much we have done in a 15-year period, and another is that we are teaching people how to develop clairvoyance. Our students don't need to be told what the health problem is; they learn to detect health problems clairvoyantly even at a distance. This is what Quimby apparently learned to do for his own use and used it until his transition. The Silva Method challenges all known systems to prove that they help humankind more than the Silva Method does.

CHAPTER 10

An Opportunity and Responsibility for Parents

The following is excerpted from José Silva's closing comments at our International Convention in Laredo, Texas, on August 9, 1998, his last major presentation just six months before his passing.

Brain Development from Conception On
by José Silva

Welcome, everybody, to this convention. I want to thank each and every one of you wonderful people for attending, graduates and non-graduates.

Now if we're going to get on a subject like the one we're working on, we need to start from some point that makes sense, because everything we do in this field is too far out for some people to be able to understand it or to accept it.

When we were born, we came from another dimension, what we call the spiritual, inanimate, subjective dimension. We call it the other side for short.

Information indicates that at a certain point in time, an intelligent human entity enters into the fetus. Sometimes they call it soul or spirit. When this happens, the brain starts functioning electronically, like transmitters and receivers. When the child starts moving in the mother's womb, it means that these electrical impulses are now taking place. There's life here, human life.

Then again, it has that special entity, a spiritual entity, that makes a difference.

An entity cannot be perceived with biological senses, yet it is the reason why the body moves. When that entity leaves, the body will not move again.

Interesting experiments have been conducted, such as:

One person who has just died, his body still warm, and another one sleeping in deep slumber, they take a cell from each of them, put the cells under a microscope, and there's no difference. Yet one can move and the other will never move again.

Something has taken off and left the one that cannot move anymore. That something we call the soul or spirit.

How the Human Brain Evolves

So we start from this dimension, entering the physical dimension at the lowest brain frequency, meaning the brain is starting to fluctuate, to pulsate, to vibrate.

Everything vibrates in the electrical magnetic spectrum. The brain starts vibrating at a very low frequency, called the delta frequency. This can be measured with an electroencephalograph (EEG), even at that stage in the mother's womb, and it puts out electrical impulses in the delta range, scientists say.

It takes the child about seven years to mature the delta and theta parts of the brain. So for seven years, the mind of the human being is functioning inductively, which means there's no human intelligence.

In other words, this mind cannot improve anything. It can function in the environment perfectly well, but cannot improve anything.

We compare this type of function with animals. All animals function inductively. They don't know how to improve anything. Birds keep on building the same nest for centuries and centuries, never improving one thing on it. Other animals build caves, and it is identical every time. All their processes are intuitively done, by instinct, they call it.

Developing Critical Consciousness

When the human being's brain matures a little higher, 7 to 14 cycles per second, scientists call it the alpha range. At that time mind changes from the inductive functioning to deductive functioning.

This is when human intelligence comes on the scene, detecting differences and being able to improve. That's what human intelligence does.

But it must function deductively to do so, not inductively.

Now we find that this particular part of the brain puts out the strongest brain frequency, in the center of the brain's frequency spectrum, at 10 cycles per second.

SCALE OF BRAIN EVOLUTION

©Copyright 1969-2001 by Jose Silva & Silva UltraMind Systems, LLC, Laredo, Texas U.S.A.

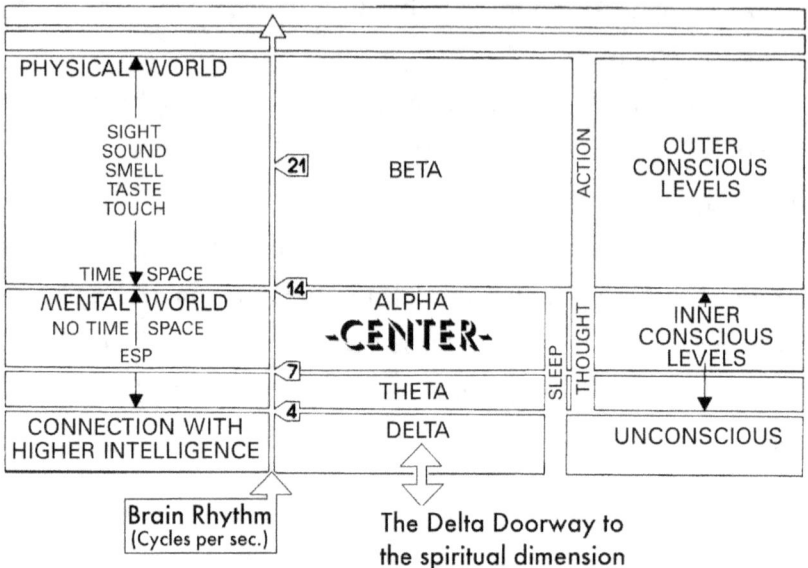

Brain Rhythm
(Cycles per sec.)

The Delta Doorway to
the spiritual dimension

Bypassing an Essential Step

When the child is born, it starts using its biological senses. The most important sense the child develops is a sense of sight. The child is attracted to everything. When the child starts reaching for something, more information is being added. The focusing faculty is being developed. They have to focus in on something and grab it.

The focusing faculty requires 20 cycles of brain function, which is in the beta brain frequency range.

So a child, while learning between 7 and 14 years of age, continues to learn by seeing first.

We think that that's the sense that throws us off from developing correctly, because you got stuck on using mostly the beta instead of the alpha frequencies.

As a result, alpha became dormant and beta became the strongest sense to focus on.

To see, we need to focus our eyes, and to focus, we need to get our brain functioning on 20 vibrations.

That kept us from developing alpha.

We should have developed alpha first, before the beta, but because of the focusing faculty—the sense of sight—we were misled.

Alpha became dormant, and beta became very active.

This is where the problem started, developing the wrong part of the brain, the left brain.

How the Brain Stores Information

The brain has a biological set of senses that records information on the left brain hemisphere, and a duplicate is transferred to the right brain.

The right brain hemisphere has a set of senses also, subjective—non-physical—senses, functioning in that dimension, and records information on the right brain but does not transfer a duplicate to the left brain.

So we always have more information on the right brain hemisphere than on the left, because we are recording information with two sets of senses on the right and only one set of senses on the left.

Since we bypassed alpha and developed consciousness in the beta only, we matured without developing the ability to function at alpha consciously.

Since we didn't develop it and are unable to use it, we call it the subconscious.

So there's twice as much information impressed in the subconscious, below the threshold of consciousness, and we cannot reach it.

Why Some People Are Lucky

Only 10 percent of humanity somehow got to develop their senses in the proper order. They were luckier because: they were more times right than wrong on decision-making, healthier because they did not attract psychosomatic health problems, and also safer because they were not accident-prone.

A person who's not able to use their information in the right brain hemisphere is the opposite: They're more accident-prone, they contract the psychosomatic health problem, and they're more times wrong than right.

Being more times right than wrong is success in itself because the more problems you solve, the more successful you are. The fewer problems you're able to solve, you're not so lucky then. You suffer because of not functioning correctly.

How to Be More Successful

So we started researching in these areas, and developed some mental training exercises—we call it mental gymnastics—to lower the brain frequency consciously to alpha, to establish a connection to the right brain and get that information that's in the subconscious, and use it, if we need to, for problem-solving.

Mind can then become attuned to alpha and operate from alpha and become aware—conscious—of the information in the "subconscious."

What we discovered was a way to change the subconscious to inner conscious. Now you have more information to use for problem-solving, and you become healthier, luckier, and safer, and that's success.

Our discovery was verified by scientists at Trinity University, at the University of Texas Medical School Health Center in San Antonio.

Why We Are Not More Successful

It all points to the idea that the Creator gave us two brain hemispheres to survive on this planet: the right one to think with, and the left one to act with.

But 90 percent of humanity were using only the left one to think and act with. It's saturated. They couldn't get any more out of it.

Maybe because of that, in desperation, we've gone in the wrong direction, in the direction of degeneration and destruction, stealing and hurting each other like animals. I think this is because we're lacking the spiritual factor. That's the right brain.

Right brain is a spiritual, subjective, non-physical, functioning type of dimension.

You need balance to function the way we should function. And the way we appear to need to function is to work on our mission assigned to us, a mission assigned to humanity.

Our Mission on Earth

The only mission we can think of is to improve living conditions on planet Earth, to help the Creator in refining creation and bring it to the final point of evolution.

We are at this end of it, to accomplish this work, and we're not doing that. We're doing just the opposite.

We're poisoning the water we drink, poisoning the air we breathe and the Earth that gives us food for survival. And destroying and hurting each other. Drugs and all this nonsense. Many babies without fathers and so on. Degeneration.

We need to enhance the spiritual factor to achieve balance. Now people are fighting each other. All the wars are religions fighting one against the other. Think about Belfast. Catholics killing Protestants and vice versa. Isn't that interesting?

They are fighting each other instead of taking this time to develop the spiritual faculty of human beings, which is their job.

In Bosnia with three different factions, religions fighting each other.

In Israel, the same thing I've seen it in Israel. When I went over there, an individual who took us around said, "Welcome to the Holy Land." What was holy about it? The people are killing each other.

Religions should be concentrating on developing what's missing in the human being: the spiritual factor, right brain thinking.

Right brain is a spiritual brain, a subjective brain. And we need to function within that dimension as well as we're functioning in the objective, physical, biological dimension, and bringing balance.

We Need a More Spiritual World

You people have experienced some of this. And you're in charge now of helping people accomplish that. We don't care if you call it religion or not—just do it. The results will be proof enough that it is possible because everybody succeeds. We want to gain helping others gain, not gain at somebody else's loss.

But this is a tremendous job because right now we have over a thousand lecturers worldwide in 107 countries, teaching in 29 languages. And it is estimated we have only trained about 15 million people. I mean, what is that against five billion plus? A drop in the bucket.

We need to do more and faster. We want to straighten out the direction that humanity is taking.

Now we have to find means and ways of training more instructors, lecturers, going to all the countries in the world.

But then again, another thought came to mind:

A Bold New Idea

Why not fathers and mothers, to teach their own children?

Once they become clairvoyant, they can take over in helping to develop the future of humanity. Papa and Mama can do it if they're fully developed clairvoyants.

The newcomers will all be trained by their parents.

That's the way it should be.

We think we have something going and we're trying to come up with ideas how to do this faster because we're too slow. We've been in this field for about thirty-five years and have trained

15 million, which is just a drop in the bucket compared to five billion plus that we need to help.

So now, for the time being, the more graduates we can train, the better off we're going to be. But we need to work together:

Instructors doing their thing, and the papas and mamas doing their thing and training their own children.

Silva instructors can help the papas and mamas to understand how to go about it.

Parents Are the Experts

In other words, Papa and Mama are the experts of what the child should be able to do because they got here first. They have more experience.

Sometimes the child doesn't think that way. They think they know it all. "Papa, he's an old-timer, he's moved too far back in time. This is a modern world, you know." That's what they think.

Papa and Mama always know more than their offspring, whether you believe it or not.

Besides that, in the spiritual dimension, the mama has all the power over them. The mother has a spiritual connection to the offspring that she can control her child, but she must know she has it and must know how to do it or else it's not going to work. It happens in a spiritual dimension. Right brain, alpha again. That channel is for that purpose.

If Mama knows that they have this faculty and knows how to use it, she can control that son or daughter who is getting into trouble.

Part 3
Universal ESP Training

CHAPTER 11

How to Activate Your Dormant Psychic Senses

by José Silva

To help you get the idea of what we are doing, we use a model of left brain/right brain functioning, as follows:

When you are at your level and visualizing and imagining (thinking about what things look like), you are impressing those experiences on both your left and your right brain hemispheres.

This happens because when you are at your level, at the alpha level, there is a connection with the right brain hemisphere. You are synchronizing the two brain hemispheres.

The left brain hemisphere stores information you detect with your physical senses—eyesight, hearing, smell, taste, and touch—and transfers copy to the right brain hemisphere.

The right brain hemisphere stores information you detect with your mental (psychic) senses, but it doesn't transfer a copy to the left hemisphere unless you are functioning at the alpha brainwave level when you detect that information.

So in order to make conscious use of the information you detect with your mental senses, you first need to learn to function at the alpha level. (Note: We will cover that in the next chapter.)

Start with What You Already Know

The first thing you do in the ESP training is to recall experiences already stored on your left brain hemisphere. You do this by recalling what your house looks like, outside and inside.

You recall these stored experiences at your level, and you transfer them to your right brain hemisphere.

Then the next thing you do is use your imagination to sense information with your subjective senses, with your right brain hemisphere, and you store these new experiences on both brain hemispheres.

In the ESP training, when you project into your living room wall, into the metals, into the leaves and to the pet, you are storing experiences on your right brain hemisphere.

When you study human anatomy from a psychic point of view, you do the same thing. You recall a relative or friend and, while at your level, transfer these memories—this stored information—to your right brain hemisphere.

Then you sense information subjectively and store this on both brain hemispheres.

Now you have points of reference on your right brain hemisphere that you will use when working health cases of people you do not know.

Putting Your New Talent to Work

When you begin working health cases, you begin with information on your right brain hemisphere, using your subjective (psychic) senses, and you transfer it to your left brain hemisphere when you describe the problems you are detecting with your mind.

You might notice that after doing a mental training exercise, you do not talk about your experiences immediately afterwards.

However, it is all right to talk about those experiences after you have gone through at least one sleep and dream cycle. You want to have this time so that while you are sleeping, your brain can properly file away the new information.

Talking about it before you have had a chance to sleep on it is like digging up a seed. You need time to internalize it.

But working health cases is different.

Since you are reporting on information that comes to you subjectively, experiences that are impressed first on your right brain hemisphere, then the process of reporting these experiences helps transfer the information to the left brain hemisphere also.

This is one of the reasons it is important to tell your orientologist everything that you think of or experience while working cases.

Using ESP Naturally

In the beginning, if you desire to use your right brain hemisphere, you must enter your level and call on the experiences you have already stored on your right brain hemisphere as you went through the Silva ESP training.

But as you store more and more experiences on your right brain hemisphere, an interesting phenomenon takes place:

You begin to develop the ability to use both brain hemispheres without closing your eyes (provided your vision is defocused) and without having to use the standard 3 to 1 method to enter your level.

Your brain automatically dips into alpha approximately 30 times every minute. This is true for all people, whether they are Silva graduates or not.

The brain stays at alpha for only a very short period of time, but this time can be very useful if you have points of reference to work with on the right brain hemisphere.

With practice, you can learn to make those brief trips to alpha last longer.

If you have not stored any experiences on your right brain hemisphere, which you do by visualizing and imagining while at the alpha level, then you will be unable to do any right brain thinking during these brief trips to alpha, because you do not have any points of reference (experiences) to guide you.

But after you have stored experiences with your right brain hemisphere, then you can begin to develop the ability to use your right brain hemisphere for thinking when your brain dips into alpha for those fractions of a second.

You can sense information with your subjective senses when your brain dips into alpha, but only if you have points of reference (experiences) on your right brain hemisphere to guide you, and you learn to recognize that special feeling of being at alpha and stay longer than that brief instant.

Start at the Beginning: Alpha

Note: In the next chapter there are several ways you can learn to enter the alpha level. After you have practiced entering the alpha level several times then you can move on to the following chapters.

It is important that you go through all of these lessons in order, because each one builds on what you experienced previously.

It is okay to go back and repeat any lessons, but no skipping forward.

CHAPTER 12

Silva Centering Exercise/Use Alpha Consciously

In order to expand your consciousness so that you can use the subconscious with conscious awareness, you need to do two things:

- Lower your brain frequency from its fully awake 20 cycles per second vibration rate to 10 cycles per second alpha frequency range.
- Then stay in alpha and not go to the lower theta and delta frequencies associated with hypnosis and deep sleep.

José Silva found a simple way to do that. It involves a combination of classical conditioning along with something he learned from hypnosis.

Since your brain is already accustomed to going to alpha under certain circumstances, he hypothesized he could expand on that ability.

Going to Alpha Naturally

When does the brain slow to alpha?

When you go to sleep.

What do you do before you go to sleep?

- You find a comfortable position
- Close your eyes
- Relax physically and mentally

When you do that, your brain frequency starts slowing down ... and ... you go to sleep.

What can stop you from going to sleep but allow you to remain at the alpha level?

The same thing that kept his hypnosis subjects from going to sleep:

Provide a small amount of mental activity that will let you remain at the alpha frequency, but not something interesting enough to bring you back to the higher beta frequencies.

We give you simple tasks like visualizing tranquil and passive scenes.

We ask you to repeat beneficial statements, for instance.

But at the very beginning we don't ask you to solve any problems.

This small amount of mental activity will help you stay at alpha and avoid continuing to lower frequencies.

Once you have learned to follow our simple instructions and remain at alpha, then it is easy for you to learn to analyze information and develop solutions while remaining at alpha.

Using the Silva Centering Exercise

What we just described is the Silva Centering Exercise (previously known as the Long Relaxation Exercise).

It is a "conditioning cycle" and "conditions" you to be able to relax physically and mentally and enter the alpha level in a matter of seconds.

You need to do more than just listen:

You need to follow the instructions in the conditioning cycle. Do what the instructor guides you to do.

In the Silva Centering Exercise, we ask you to make yourself comfortable, close your eyes, and relax your body from head to toes. Then we associate this physical relaxation to the number 3.

Then we guide you to relax mentally and associate mental relaxation to the number 2.

As you continue to follow the simple instructions, your brain will be at the alpha frequency. We associate this with the number 1.

After you have practiced a few times, you will be able to enter the alpha level in a few seconds by mentally repeating and visualizing the numbers with the intention of entering alpha. You will simply:

- Take a deep breath and while exhaling, mentally repeat and visualize the number 3 three times, and relax physically.
- Take another deep breath and while exhaling, mentally repeat and visualize the number 2 three times, and relax mentally.
- Take another deep breath and while exhaling, mentally repeat and visualize the number 1 three times, and take it for granted that you have entered the alpha level.

Stay positive. Take it for granted you are at the correct level.

Some people report that being at the alpha level is similar to how they feel when they first wake up from a restful night's sleep.

The fastest way to learn is to have someone guide you through the Silva Centering Exercise. You can have somebody read it to you or record it for you, or listen to a CD or mp3 audio, or steam it online, or you can record it yourself. The script is below.

You can start right now with the Free Introductory Lessons at the SilvaNow.com website or the SilvaNow Course at our youtube.com/@SilvaMindVideo channel.

Another Option

There is another way to learn, one that Mr. Silva included in the books that he wrote before we had the capability of streaming audio on the internet. If you don't have a way to listen to the Centering Exercise, you may find it easier than memorizing the steps in the Centering Exercise:

You can practice countdown deepening exercises every morning for 40 days, starting with 100 to 1 for the first 10 days. Then you shorten the countdowns and add some beneficial statements and other elements. The instructions are in Appendix C.

Please note: This is optional, an alternative to the Centering Exercise. You do not need to do both; just do whatever works best for you.

Either way the idea is the same: Remain at alpha with conscious awareness.

A Unique Type of Meditation

Other types of meditation that direct you to repeat a mantra or visualize a candle flame, for instance, tend to go to lower frequencies, lower than alpha. That is great for some purposes, but for problem-solving we want to be able to activate our mind at the 10 cycles alpha frequency.

You learn that with the Silva Centering Exercise.

How to Read the Silva Centering Exercise

José Silva has this advice for reading the Centering Exercise:

"When reading the Silva Centering Exercise, read in a relaxed, natural voice. Be close enough so that the listener can hear you comfortably. Read loud enough to be heard, and read as though you were reading to a seven-year-old child. Speak each word clearly and distinctly.

"Have the listener assume a comfortable position. A sitting position is preferred, but the most important thing is to make sure the listener is comfortable. If uncomfortable, the listener will not relax as much and will not get as much benefit from the exercise.

"Avoid distractions, such as loud outside noises. There should be enough light so you can read comfortably, but not extremely bright lights.

"If the person shows any signs of nervousness or appears to be uncomfortable, stop reading, tell them to relax and make themselves comfortable. When they are comfortable and ready, then continue.

"Take your time when you read; there is no need to rush."

A Quick Review:

- Sit in any position that is comfortable; let your body do what it needs to do to be comfortable. It is okay to lie down if you need to.
- If you need to readjust your position, do so; if you need to scratch, scratch.

- If you need to open your eyes, then open your eyes and make yourself comfortable, then when you are ready, close your eyes, and start again at the beginning of the exercise.
- Follow the instructions. Don't just sit passively; get involved, and let your body relax.
- To "visualize the number 3" means to recall what it looks like. Use your mind, not your physical eyesight.
- Do the same to "detect a fine vibration, a tingling sensation, a feeling of warmth." Recall a sensation like that. Do it with your mind.
- To "release and relax all tensions and ligament pressures" is like releasing your grip on something you have been holding tightly. You cannot force yourself to relax, so just let go and relax your muscles.

The Silva Centering Exercise Script

Note: Do not read the headings out loud. They are for your information.

Deepening (Physical Relaxation at Level 3)

We will start this exercise with the 3 to 1 method.

Find a comfortable position, close your eyes, take a deep breath, and, while exhaling, mentally repeat and visualize the number 3 three times. (pause)

To help you learn to relax physically at level 3, I am going to direct your attention to different parts of your body.

Concentrate your sense of awareness on your scalp, the skin that covers your head; you will detect a fine vibration, a tingling sensation, a feeling of warmth caused by circulation. (pause) Now release and completely relax all tensions and ligament pressures from this part of your head and place it in a deep state of relaxation that will grow deeper as we continue. (pause)

Concentrate your sense of awareness on your forehead, the skin that covers your forehead; you will detect a fine vibration, a tingling sensation, a feeling of warmth caused by circulation. (pause) Now release and completely relax all tensions and ligament pressures from this part of your head and place it in a deep state of relaxation that will grow deeper as we continue. (pause)

Concentrate your sense of awareness on your eyelids and the tissue surrounding your eyes; you will detect a fine vibration, a tingling sensation, a feeling of warmth caused by circulation. (pause) Now release and completely relax all tensions and ligament pressures from this part of your head and place it in a deep state of relaxation that will grow deeper as we continue. (pause)

Concentrate your sense of awareness on your face, the skin covering your cheeks; you will detect a fine vibration, a tingling sensation, a feeling of warmth caused by circulation. (pause) Now release and completely relax all tensions and ligament pressures from this part of your head and place it in a deep state of relaxation that will grow deeper as we continue. (pause)

Concentrate on the outer portion of your throat, the skin covering your throat area; you will detect a fine vibration, a tingling sensation, a feeling of warmth caused by circulation. (pause) Now release and completely relax all tensions and ligament pressures from this part of your body and place it in a deep state of relaxation that will grow deeper as we continue. (pause)

Concentrate within the throat area and relax all tensions and ligament pressures from this part of your body and place it in a deep state of relaxation, going deeper and deeper every time. (pause)

Concentrate on your shoulders; feel your clothing in contact with your body. (pause) Feel the skin and the vibration of the skin covering this part of your body. (pause) Relax all tensions and ligament pressures and place your shoulders in a deep state of relaxation, going deeper and deeper every time. (pause)

Concentrate on your chest; feel your clothing in contact with this part of your body. (pause) Feel the skin and the vibration of your skin covering your chest. (pause) Relax all tensions and ligament pressures and place your chest in a deep state of relaxation, going deeper and deeper every time. (pause)

Concentrate within the chest area; relax all organs; relax all glands; relax all tissues, including the cells themselves, and cause them to function in a rhythmic, healthy manner. (pause)

Concentrate on your abdomen; feel the clothing in contact with this part of your body. (pause) Feel the skin and the vibration of your skin covering your abdomen. (pause) Relax all tensions and ligament pressures and place your abdomen in a deep state of relaxation, going deeper and deeper every time. (pause)

Concentrate within the abdominal area; relax all organs; relax all glands; relax all tissues, including the cells themselves, and cause them to function in a rhythmic, healthy manner. (pause)

Concentrate on your thighs; feel your clothing in contact with this part of your body. (pause) Feel the skin and the vibration of your skin covering your thighs. (pause) Relax all tensions and ligament pressures and place your thighs in a deep state of relaxation, going deeper and deeper every time. (pause)

Sense the vibrations at the bones within the thighs; by now these vibrations should be easily detectable. (pause)

Concentrate on your knees; feel the skin and the vibration of your skin covering the knees. (pause) Relax all tensions and ligament pressures and place your knees in a deep state of relaxation, going deeper and deeper every time (pause)

Concentrate on your calves; feel the skin and the vibration of the skin covering your calves. (pause) Relax all tensions and ligament pressures and place these parts of your body in a deep state of relaxation, going deeper and deeper every time. (pause)

To enter a deeper, healthier level of mind, concentrate on your toes. (pause) Enter a deeper, healthier level of mind.

To enter a deeper, healthier level of mind, concentrate on the soles of your feet. (pause) Enter a deeper, healthier level of mind. (pause)

To enter a deeper, healthier level of mind, concentrate on the heels of your feet. (pause) Enter a deeper, healthier level of mind. (pause)

Now cause your feet to feel as though they do not belong to your body. (pause)

Feel your feet as though they do not belong to your body. (pause)

Your feet feel as though they do not belong to your body. (pause)

Your feet, ankles, calves, and knees feel as though they do not belong to your body. (pause)

Your feet, ankles, calves, knees, thighs, waist, shoulders, arms, and hands feel as though they do not belong to your body. (pause)

You are now at a deeper, healthier level of mind, deeper than before.

This is your physical relaxation level 3. Whenever you mentally repeat and visualize the number 3, your body will relax as completely as you are now, and more so every time you practice.

Deepening (Mental Relaxation at Level 2)

To enter the mental relaxation level 2, mentally repeat and visualize the number 2 several times, and you are at level 2, a deeper level than 3. (pause) Level 2 is for mental relaxation, where noises will not distract you. Instead, noises will help you to relax mentally more and more.

To help you learn to relax mentally at level 2, I am going to call your attention to different passive scenes. Visualizing any scene that makes you tranquil and passive will help you relax mentally.

Your being at the beach on a nice summer day may be a tranquil and passive scene for you. (pause)

A day out fishing may be a tranquil and passive scene for you. (pause)

A tranquil and passive scene for you may be a walk through the woods on a beautiful summer day, when the breeze is just right, where there are tall shade trees, beautiful flowers, a very blue sky, an occasional white cloud, birds singing in the distance, even squirrels playing on the tree limbs. Hear birds singing in the distance. (pause)

This is mental relaxation level 2, where noises will not distract you.

To enhance mental relaxation at level 2, practice visualizing tranquil and passive scenes.

To Enter Your Center

To enter level 1, mentally repeat and visualize the number 1 several times. (pause)

You are now at level 1, the basic level where you can function from your center.

Deepening Exercises

To enter deeper, healthier levels of mind, practice with the countdown deepening exercises. To deepen, count downward from 25 to 1, or from 50 to 1, or from 100 to 1. When you reach the count of 1, you will have reached a deeper, healthier level of mind, deeper than before.

You will always have full control and complete dominion over your faculties and senses at all levels of the mind, including the outer conscious level.

When to Practice

The best time to practice the countdown deepening exercises is in the morning when you wake up. Remain in bed at least five minutes practicing the countdown deepening exercises.

The second-best time to practice is at night, when you are ready to retire.

The third best time to practice is at noon after lunch.

Five minutes of practice is good; ten minutes is very good; fifteen minutes is excellent.

To practice once a day is good; two times a day is very good; and three times a day is excellent.

If you have a health problem, practice for fifteen minutes, three times a day.

To Come out of Levels

To come out of any level of the mind, count to yourself mentally from 1 to 5 and tell yourself that at the count of 5 you will open your eyes and be wide awake, feeling fine and in perfect health, feeling better than before.

Then proceed to count slowly from 1 to 2, then to 3, and at the count of 3 mentally remind yourself that at the count of 5 you will open your eyes, be wide awake, feeling fine and in perfect health, feeling better than before.

Proceed to count slowly to 4, then to 5. At the count of 5 and with your eyes open, mentally tell yourself, "I am wide awake, feeling fine, and in perfect health, feeling better than before. And this is so."

Deepening (Routine Cycle)

To help you enter a deeper, healthier level of mind, I am going to count from 10 to 1. On each descending number, you will feel yourself going deeper and you will enter a deeper, healthier level of mind.

10—9, feel going deeper,

8—7—6, deeper and deeper

5—4—3, deeper and deeper,

2—1

You are now at a deeper, healthier level of mind, deeper than before.

You may enter a deeper, healthier level of mind by simply relaxing your eyelids. Relax your eyelids. (pause) Feel how relaxed they are. (pause) Allow this feeling of relaxation to flow slowly downward throughout your body, all the way down to your toes. (pause)

It is a wonderful feeling to be deeply relaxed, a very healthy state of being.

To help you enter a deeper, healthier level of mind, I am going to count from 1 to 3. At that moment, you will project yourself mentally to your ideal place of relaxation. I will then stop talking to you, and when you next hear my voice, one hour of time will have elapsed at this level of mind. My voice will not startle you; you will take a deep breath, relax, and go deeper.

1—(pause)—2—(pause)—3. Project yourself mentally to your ideal place of relaxation until you hear my voice again. Relax. (**Instructor**: Remain silent for about 30 seconds.)

Relax. (pause) Take a deep breath and as you exhale, relax and go deeper. (pause)

Rapport

You will continue to listen to my voice; you will continue to follow the instructions at this level of the mind and any other level, including the outer conscious level. This is for your benefit; you desire it, and it is so.

Whenever you hear me mention the word "Relax," or whenever you mentally or verbally mention the word "Relax," all unnecessary movements and activities of your body, brain, and mind will cease immediately, and you will become completely passive and relaxed physically and mentally.

I may bring you out of this level or a deeper level than this by counting to you from 1 to 5. At the count of 5, your eyes will open; you will be wide awake, feeling fine and in perfect health.

I may bring you out of this level or a deeper level than this by touching your left shoulder three times. When you feel my hand touch your left shoulder for the third time, your eyes will open; you will be wide awake, feeling fine, and in perfect health. And this is so.

Genius Statements

The difference between genius mentality and lay mentality is that geniuses use more of their minds and use them in a special manner.

You are now learning to use more of your mind and to use it in a special manner.

Beneficial Statements

The following are beneficial statements that you may occasionally repeat while at these levels of the mind. Repeat mentally after me. (**Instructor**: Read slowly.)

My increasing mental faculties are for serving humanity better.

Every day, in every way, I am getting better, better, and better.

Positive thoughts bring me benefits and advantages I desire.

I will always maintain a perfectly healthy body and mind.

I have full control and complete dominion over my sensing faculties at this level of the mind and any other level, including the outer conscious level. And this is so.

Effective Sensory Projection Statements

Effective Sensory Projection statements for success:

I am now learning to attune my intelligence by developing my sensing faculties and to project them to any point or place on this planet so as to be aware of any actions taking place, if this is necessary and beneficial for humanity.

I am now learning to attune my intelligence by developing my sensing faculties and to project them to any point or place on any planet within the solar system, any solar system within the galaxy, and any galaxy within the universe so as to be aware of any actions taking place, if this is necessary and beneficial for humanity.

I am now learning to attune my intelligence by developing my sensing faculties and to project them to the different matter kingdoms: the inanimate matter kingdom, any of its levels and depths; the animate matter kingdom with reproductive intelligence, plant life and animal life, any of its levels and depths; and the animate matter kingdom with reproductive intelligence and an awareness of existence, the human body and mind kingdom, any of its levels and depths.

I am now learning to detect abnormalities whenever such abnormalities exist within any kingdom, any level, and any depth, if this is necessary and beneficial for humanity.

I am now learning to apply corrective measures and to bring back to normalcy any abnormality found within any kingdom, any level, and any depth, if this is necessary and beneficial for humanity.

Negative thoughts and negative suggestions have no influence over me at any level of the mind.

Post Effects: Preview of Next Session

You have practiced entering deep, healthy levels of mind. In your next session, you will enter a deeper, healthier level of mind, faster and easier than this time.

Post Effects: Standard

Every time you function at these levels of the mind, you will receive beneficial effects physically and mentally.

You may use these levels of the mind to help yourself physically and mentally.

You may use these levels of the mind to help your loved ones, physically and mentally.

You may use these levels of the mind to help any human being who needs help, physically and mentally.

You will never use these levels of the mind to harm any human being; if this be your intention, you will not be able to function within these levels of the mind.

You will always use these levels of the mind in a constructive, creative manner for all that is good, honest, pure, clean, and positive. And this is so.

You will continue to strive to take part in constructive and creative activities to make this a better world to live in, so that when we move on, we shall have left behind a better world for those who follow. You will consider the whole of humanity, depending on their ages, as fathers or mothers, brothers or sisters, sons or daughters. You are a superior human being; you have greater understanding, compassion, and patience with others.

Bring Out

In a moment, I am going to count from 1 to 5. At that moment, you will open your eyes, be wide awake, feeling fine and in perfect health, feeling better than before. You will have no ill effects whatsoever in your head, no headache; no ill effects whatsoever in your hearing, no buzzing in your ears; no ill effects whatsoever in your vision and eyesight; vision, eyesight, and hearing improve every time you function at these levels of mind.

1–2, coming out slowly now.

3, at the count of 5, you will open your eyes, be wide awake, feeling fine and in perfect health, feeling better than before, feeling the way you feel when you have slept the right amount of revitalizing, refreshing, relaxing, healthy sleep.

4–5, eyes open, wide awake, feeling fine and in perfect health, feeling better than before.

(**Reader**: Be sure to observe whether or not the person is wide awake. If in doubt, touch the person's left shoulder three times and while doing so say: "Wide awake, feeling fine and in perfect health. And this is so.")

It is recommended that everyone practice staying at their center for 15 minutes a day to normalize all abnormal conditions of the body and mind.

If you would like to share this experience with family members, friends, and associates, please see the Save the Planet Project in Appendix B.

CHAPTER 13

Procedure to Develop Superior ESP

In the previous lesson you learned to enter the alpha brain wave level with conscious awareness. This is a prerequisite to learning to develop superior ESP.

You can learn to enter the alpha level with the Silva Centering Exercise in the previous chapter, or the Alternative Method in Appendix C.

Other forms of meditation, including yoga and Zen and others, have a different goal. They go to lower frequencies. So it is important to use our system when you are learning.

Once you have had success with our system, then it is okay to experiment with other modalities if you wish, because you will have a baseline to compare your results with other techniques with the known results you get with our system.

With that in mind, let's see what comes next:

Silva UltraMind ESP System Best Practices

To obtain the fastest and best results, José Silva advised us to continue to practice with the Silva Centering Exercise. That is incorporated into the course structure, as you can see in the course syllabus in the next chapter.

The procedure we use in live classes and webinars involves three steps:

First, practice the Centering Exercise.

Then we explain the procedure of the next conditioning cycle. That is known as the preconditioning.

We follow that with a conditioning cycle with mental projection exercises—José Silva called them "mental calisthenics"—to establish points of reference in the subjective (mental) dimension.

Points of Reference

Points of reference are anything that can help you recognize where you are.

If you are giving someone directions to your home, you might tell them to "turn right at the traffic light, go two blocks more, and the big white house on the corner is my house." Those physical "points of reference" make it easy for them to find your house.

You already have objective points of reference for your home, information you have detected with your physical senses. This information is impressed on your left brain hemisphere.

In the Projection to Home exercise, you will go to the alpha level and then review the objective impressions of your home, both outside and inside the building.

Then you will do something you cannot do with your physical senses: project your mind into your living room wall, into the material it is made of—wood, wallboard, metal, concrete blocks, bricks. You will imagine going right into it.

Then you will start establishing subjective points of reference by conducting four tests:

- Light, intensity, and color
- Temperature
- Odor
- Solidity of material by reflected sound

It doesn't matter what you detect, because these points of reference are for your benefit. They are your way of synchronizing your subjective senses with your objective impressions.

Perhaps in the future you are shopping for a new home. If you want to verify what material it is made of—and if it really is in as good condition as the seller claims—you can project into it mentally and search for any problem areas.

In the next mental projection exercise, you will establish points of reference in the inanimate matter kingdom, at the molecular level. You will project yourself into several metallic items and run the same tests as you did inside the wall.

In the mental projection exercise after that, you will move up to the cell level. You will study a tree subjectively, then project yourself mentally into leaves from two different plants.

These three mental projection exercises prepare you to function mentally within any kingdom, including the animal and human kingdoms, which we will do in the final two mental projection exercises.

If you are eager to get started, you can go directly to the next chapter and follow the instructions.

If you want to hear from the leading expert in this field as he explains it as only he can, then continue with the rest of this chapter.

José Silva Reveals How His ESP System Works
by José Silva

Once the student finds the alpha dimension, then we need to get them to become familiar with this dimension. In order for the person to become familiar, we need to go over what the person already knows, what the person has experienced, so they will not jump into something new altogether.

How do we do this?

We want to first get them to use their mind, meaning their human intelligence, at this dimension, at the 10-cycle frequency, and go over what the person has learned and experienced.

What does the person have in mind as experiences? Well, what do you do more per day? You know how to dress yourself, you live in a certain home, you've seen this home many times, you know your bedroom, you know your living room, you know your kitchen at home. It depends on how long you've lived in this particular place.

Let's go over and review what you have learned, what you have accumulated in your brain as information. We want to go over—not with the left brain hemisphere—but now with the right one because you are now at 10 cycles per second brain activity.

Let's call it mental projection. Now mentally project yourself to be standing in front of your home and look at your house. You've seen this so many times.

Look at the roof. Remember the roof. What type of roof do you have?

Come down from top to bottom—like reading a book: from left to right—and go over everything. It attracts your attention, so describe it mentally. You've seen it before. You're recording what experiences you have.

Windows? Are they painted different colors? What colors are your windows?

We go over with the student, give them enough time to look at these different parts of their house and to notice colors. Make sure you detect colors.

What color is your roof, what color are the windows, what color is your house, the leaves of the tree if you have a tree in front of your house, and so on. Colors, colors, colors. Always want to bring in colors. This is the spectrum of this dimension.

Then you walk toward the front door. You've walked toward the door so many times, it's strongly impressed on your brain. You have no trouble in recalling what you have seen before because it's like remembering.

You Are Using Visualization

Remembering is visualizing. Remembering what you have seen is visualizing.

You're already practicing visualization with the use of the right brain hemisphere.

You've done it, but you did it before with the left brain hemisphere. You're not getting too many things done with the left one. We want to do more things with the right one in addition to the left one.

You have learned to use the left brain hemisphere. Now we are teaching you to use the right one.

Copy Your Experiences to the Right Brain

Let's go and make a copy of everything you've seen, all your experiences, and transfer them consciously to your right brain hemisphere now, consciously.

Imagine walking toward your door. Remember what kind of door handle you have? Is it round? You know what it is; you've seen it before.

You've touched it so many times. Feel as though you're touching it again. You're opening the door, the front door to enter your home using your key. If you have a key and you want to unlock the door. You've done it many times, now go over it mentally.

This is mental projection through visualization, learning to use the right brain hemisphere. You have done this so many times but while using the left one, so now we want to transfer all that information to the right to get started in learning to use the right brain hemisphere.

Once you get inside the house, close the door behind you. Now, stand in the center of your living room. We want you to face the south wall. You know which is south. It doesn't matter where your body is facing—north or east or west—but mentally, we want you to face south.

Now, concentrate on the south wall in your living room. You can do that. You've been here before.

You've been here during the daytime. You know what kind of light enters what window and what you have in front of you, what furniture is to your left, what furniture is to your right, what furniture is behind you.

You've been here at night when the lights are turned on.

You've been here in your living room at night when the lights are turned off.

We want to establish all information that has previously been recorded and impressed, experienced, with the left brain hemisphere.

When you do this at the 10 cycles alpha level, you automatically transfer the information to the right hemisphere. This is the very beginning of developing your ESP.

Now You Are Ready for the Next Step

The next step is to start doing things you've never done before. We start creating new ideas.

For instance, we mentioned for you to be standing in the center of your living room facing the south wall.

Then we instruct you to imagine walking toward the south wall. You want to touch the south wall with your hand.

Now we are adding something that maybe you have never done before. Maybe you never walked toward the south wall and extended your arm and placed the palm of your hand on the south wall.

Now you are doing it mentally.

You didn't have this point of reference with the left brain hemisphere.

Creating New Subjective Points of Reference

We're able to set new points of reference now, which means using your imagination. If you have not done it before, you're not going over past experiences, you're not recording what you have seen or done, you're doing it for the first time in this dimension. You need to imagine it.

Mentally creating something or doing something for the first time, that you've never done, is imagination.

So we instruct you to touch the wall. Get the feel of it.

Is it rough? Is it smooth?

Is it cold? Is it warm or hot?

You are getting more of your senses involved—the sense of touch, for instance—and we say that whatever you imagine that it is like, this is what it is for you here in this dimension.

Then we expand a little more. We want to keep on doing more and more things that you have never done before even with the left brain hemisphere.

For instance, imagine that you get closer and closer to the wall. You're about arm's length. Now, a foot away, 12 inches (30 centimeters) away. Now you're three inches (7.5 centimeters) away.

Focus on the wall. You can see the pores of the wood, or brick if it's brick or cement. Concentrate on it, establishing points of reference for the first time.

More Information Available to Your Mind

Now, go ahead and project yourself mentally inside the wall. You've never been inside this wall physically. Imagine that you are. Use your imagination.

Now, here, inside the wall, this is the first time you have experienced this. Tell me, is there any sense of sight to be used here? Is there any light? Try and see if you can detect anything. What do you imagine that you would see inside the wall? Whatever your imagination perceives at this dimension, this is what it would be for you in the future as an experience, a point of reference.

In other words, we are establishing points of reference with the imagination. This is a fundamental basic point of reference.

We're going to get more complex in the later exercises. Then you will be able to find oil if you need to. Where is the oil? How deep is it?

What quadrants are there to find gold, for instance? You know where the gold vein is for finding gold if you have experiences of observing gold in the mental dimension, while you are at the 10 cycles alpha brainwave frequency.

Learn Like a Child

Your mind can do anything, but first you need to establish your points of reference. Then if you find something, discover something, you will be able to identify it because you have a previous experience to correlate with it.

The mental dimension is an existing world just as much as the physical dimension is, so you need to establish points of reference in each of them.

When a child touches the toy and later touches it again, they can know what it is, even with their eyes closed, once they have a previous experience in touching it and how it felt. They don't have to see it to know that it's a toy. With eyes closed they will guess correctly, because they have a previous experience.

First the Basics, Then More Complex

It's the same thing here. When you start establishing points of reference or initial points of reference, you develop initial experiences with as many things as we can think of in the inanimate world, the molecular dimension.

Then we do the same in the animate world, where we find cells and organs and organ systems.

We say inanimate world physics, animate vegetable, animate animal, animate human. We want to establish points of reference in every kingdom.

First of all, we must function in the inanimate world, the inanimate kingdom, and establish as many points of reference as we can, like we do when we project into the wall.

We tell you, "Now you are inside the wall. Imagine that you are. You've never been here before, but now, using your subjective sense of sight—not your physical eyesight, use your imagination—do you detect any brilliance here? Any light? If so, what intensity, and if so, what color?"

Whatever your imagination perceives, this is what it would be for you as a point of reference for the future because you are experiencing that right now.

"What do you imagine that you can perceive?"

Then we say sense of smell. Is there a difference of smell inside this wall as compared to being outside? Use your imagination. Then this is mental projection to the wall, for instance.

Now sound. What are we going to know about sound? Form a fist, an imaginary fist, and knock on the inside of the wall and imagine how the sound reflects to you.

Is it very solid? Whatever your imagination perceives as a reflection from what you're doing is what you will use as a point of reference in the future with your mind.

All of these subjective senses belong to the right brain hemisphere.

The objective senses belong to the left hemisphere. They are extensions of the fundamental—subjective—senses.

Moving Up to More Complex Dimensions

Once we do all of this, you are starting to develop the use of your imagination at the 10-cycle dimension using the right brain hemisphere.

Then we move into other areas of inanimate matter, detection of metal. We will objectively bring into class pieces of metal: stainless steel, copper, brass, aluminum. We give you time to become familiar with each metal with your physical senses: to touch them, smell the different metals, smell the stainless steel, smell the copper.

In other words, objectively establish initial points of reference in the world of the left brain hemisphere.

Once you have established the use of all your physical senses—how it feels, how it smells, how it tastes, whatever you want to do—then we project into the mental dimension.

You will enter the alpha level and imagine that you're holding the piece of stainless steel in your hand. Imagine that you're bringing it closer to your forehead. Remember what you did before; play back those points of reference.

Once we have established those experiences in the left brain hemisphere, we transfer them to the right hemisphere.

At 10 cycles alpha, you are taking those impressions and establishing them in the right brain hemisphere dimension. You go over the same thing again. You imagine feeling the piece of metal. You have touched your forehead with it, because this is what we instructed you to do.

Now, how much farther can you go from here?

Physically, you cannot go any further in touching the piece of metal to your forehead. But mentally, you are going to project inside the stainless steel.

Now that you are inside the stainless steel, use your imagination. What kind of light or amount of light, color of light, do you detect here? Whatever you imagine, that's what counts here.

You do the same things you did inside the wall: the intensity of light, the color of light inside the stainless steel, the way it smells, the sounds when you knock on the inside with your bare knuckles, and so on. All of this is impressed, so that you establish your points of reference.

There are more exercises to be done within the wall, with the stainless steel, with copper, brass, and aluminum.

Then we compare them with each other.

Then in the next mental training exercise we move up to the animate matter kingdom. You will study two leaves in the same way and then project into the leaves.

In later exercises you will study the anatomy of a pet and human anatomy from a psychic point of view.

CHAPTER 14

Course Syllabus

We present the training in two eight-hour days in our in-person classes. Live webinars run about 16 hours total time. The Silva UltraMind ESP System Complete Home Seminar is a couple of hours longer.

  1: Silva Centering Exercise—25 minutes

  2: Mental Projection to Home—39 minutes

  3: Silva Centering Exercise—25 minutes

  4: Mental Projection into Metals—39 minutes

  5: Silva Centering Exercise—25 minutes

  6: Mental Projection—into Plant Life—31 minutes

  7: Silva Centering Exercise—25 minutes

  8: Mental Projection into Animal Life—26 minutes

  9: Practice Psychometry

10: Silva Centering Exercise—25 minutes

11: Mental Projection into Human Life—39 minutes

12: Practice Detection and Correction of Problem Cases at a Distance

CHAPTER 15

Mental Projection to Home

Prerequisite: Silva Centering Exercise

Now that you have learned how to enter the alpha level, you can begin reactivating your dormant right brain hemisphere.

The first step in reactivating your right brain hemisphere is to enter the alpha level, where you have access to both brain hemispheres.

Then you will review impressions you have made on your left brain hemisphere with your physical senses to those impressions with your right brain hemisphere.

Next you will use your imagination to make new impressions on your right brain hemisphere.

You can listen to a recording of this exercise, or have somebody read it to you, or you can enter your level and do the mental projection drills on your own.

Please read through the "Impression of New Material" first, before you go to your level, so you will know what to expect. This is known as "preconditioning."

Allow yourself enough time to complete the entire exercise, about 37 minutes. Turn off all communications devices, hang a "Do not disturb" sign on the door, ask people not to disturb you. You need to go through the entire exercise. The "Post Effects" at the end are special instructions for your brain, and they must be included.

It is like baking a cake: If you leave out one of the ingredients, you can't go back and add it later after the cake is baked; you have to start over again from the beginning.

Some people find that having a "Mental Screen" helps them to visualize and imagine mental images, so we include that for those who find it useful. The Mental Screen is out and away from your body, about 20 degrees above horizontal relative to your face.

After we complete the mental projection exercises, we will program two formula-type techniques:

The 3-Scenes Technique to help you use your mind to correct problems.

The MentalVideo to request help and guidance from higher intelligence when you are stuck.

You can read more about those two techniques in Chapter 7.

The format is the same for each conditioning cycle:

- Enter level with the 3 to 1 method.
- Deepen with a 10 to 1 countdown.
- Program new information
- Post Effects
- Bring Out by counting from 1 to 5.

Now here is the complete Projection to Home exercise:

Projection to Home Mental Exercise

(Note: Do not read the headings out loud. They are for the reader's benefit only.)

DEEPENING (physical relaxation at level 3)

We will start this exercise with the 3 to 1 method.

Find a comfortable position, close your eyes, take a deep breath, and while exhaling, mentally repeat and visualize the number 3 three times. (pause)

To help you learn to relax physically at level 3, I am going to direct your attention to different parts of your body.

(**Instructor**: Pause after every mention.)

Relax your scalp; relax your forehead; relax your eyes; relax your face; relax your throat; relax your shoulders; relax your chest externally and internally; relax your abdominal area externally and internally; relax your thighs; relax your knees; relax your calves; relax your feet.

You are now at a deeper, healthier level of mind, deeper than before.

This is your physical relaxation level 3. Whenever you mentally repeat and visualize the number 3, your body will relax as completely as you are now, and more so every time you practice.

DEEPENING (mental relaxation at level 2)

To enter mental relaxation level 2, take a deep breath, and while exhaling mentally repeat and visualize the number 2 three times, and you are at level 2, a deeper level than 3. (pause) Level 2 is for mental relaxation, where noises will not distract you. Instead, noises will help you to relax mentally more and more.

To improve mental relaxation at level 2, practice visualizing tranquil and passive scenes. (pause)

TO ENTER YOUR CENTER

Take another deep breath and while exhaling, mentally repeat and visualize number 1 three times. (pause)

You are now at level 1, a deeper, healthier level of mind where you can function from your center.

DEEPENING (routine cycle)

To help you enter a deeper, healthier level of mind, I am going to count from 10 to 1. On each descending number, you will feel yourself going deeper and you will enter a deeper, healthier level of mind.

10—9—feel going deeper,

8—7—6—deeper and deeper,

5—4—3—deeper and deeper,

2—1

You are now at a deeper, healthier level of mind, deeper than before.

It is a wonderful feeling to be deeply relaxed, a very healthy state of being.

EFFECTIVE SENSORY PROJECTION STATEMENTS

Effective Sensory Projection statements for success.

I am now learning to attune my intelligence by developing my sensing faculties and to project them to any point or place on this planet so as to be aware of any actions taking place, if this is necessary and beneficial for humanity.

I am now learning to attune my intelligence by developing my sensing faculties and to project them to any point or place on any planet within the solar system, any solar system within the galaxy, and any galaxy within the universe so as to be aware of any actions taking place, if this is necessary and beneficial for humanity.

I am now learning to attune my intelligence by developing my sensing faculties and to project them to the different matter kingdoms: the inanimate matter kingdom, any of its levels and depths; the animate matter kingdom with reproductive intelligence, plant life and animal life, any of its levels and depths; and the animate matter kingdom with reproductive intelligence and an awareness of existence, the human body and mind kingdom, any of its levels and depths.

I am now learning to detect abnormalities whenever such abnormalities exist within any kingdom, any level, and any depth, if this is necessary and beneficial for humanity.

I am now learning to apply corrective measures and to bring back to normalcy any abnormality found within any kingdom, any level, and any depth, if this is necessary and beneficial for humanity.

Negative thoughts and negative suggestions have no influence over me at any level of the mind.

LAWS OF PROGRAMMING

The following laws are to be considered when programming:

You should do to others only what you like others to do to you.

The solution must help to make this planet a better place to live.

It must be the best for everybody concerned.

It must help at least two or more persons.

It must be within the possibility area.

PRINCIPLES TO KEEP IN MIND WHEN PROGRAMMING

The following principles apply to programming.

Objective physical communication takes place at the beta, left brain dimension using the objective—physical—senses. The hearing is used for perception, and the voice is used for transmission.

Subjective—mental—communication takes place at your center, the alpha, right brain dimension by using the subjective senses. Visualization is used for perception, and imagination is used for transmission.

In the objective—physical—dimension, the past is behind us, the present is our present position, and the future is ahead of us.

In the subjective—mental—dimension, the past is to your right, the present is centered straight ahead, and the future is to your left.

PROGRAMMING THE MENTAL SCREEN

We will now impress new information for your benefit: the Mental Screen. To locate your Mental Screen, begin with your eyes closed, turned slightly upward from the horizontal plane of sight, at an angle of approximately 20 degrees. The area that you perceive with your mind is your Mental Screen.

Without using your eyelids as screens, sense your Mental Screen to be out, away from your body. To improve the use of your Mental Screen, project images or mental pictures onto the screen, especially images having color. Concentrate on mentally sensing and visualizing true color.

PROJECTION TO HOME

We will now program Effective Sensory Projection for your success. We will program information through the use of mental projection. We will establish subjective points of reference at the imaginative dimension, the subjective dimension, at different levels and depths.

In a moment I am going to count from 1 to 3 and cause a sound with my fingers. At that time, you will imagine yourself to be standing about 30 feet in front of your home. You will study the outer appearance of your home, scanning the scene.

You will start at the top left of the scene and go from left to right, just as you do when reading a page of a book. You will then go to the left side of the scene again, but a little lower than before, and again go from left to right; you will continue going a little lower each time until you reach the ground level.

I will now count from 1 to 3 and cause a sound with my fingers so that you may imagine projecting yourself to the front of your home. 1—2—3 (snap fingers). Project yourself mentally to the front of your home, standing about 30 feet from it. Begin scanning the scene at the upper left-hand corner, going slowly from left to right, lower each time until you reach the ground level.

You will go slowly and stop to study anything that attracts your intelligence while scanning, such as the roof, windows, window frames, doors. Study anything that attracts you.

Begin by studying the roof of your home. (pause) What material is it made of? (pause) What color is it? (pause) Continue studying everything that attracts you, until you reach the ground level. Concentrate on colors.

(**Instructor**: Allow about 1 minute for this, occasionally saying: "Take your time," "Study colors.")

Scan the ground level. (pause) Now, focus your attention on the front door, and concentrate on the doorknob or handle. Mentally move close to the door, close enough to touch the door handle; expect the door to appear to increase in size as you get closer. (pause) Mentally touch the doorknob or handle, open the door; mentally enter your home, closing the door behind you. (pause)

Mentally walk toward your living room; once you have entered your living room, stand at the center, facing the south wall. (pause) You have been here before; you have been here during daylight hours; you have been here during nighttime, with the lights turned on, and lights turned off.

I am going to count from 1 to 3; at the count of 3 it will be daytime. 1—2—3 (snap fingers). It is now daytime; you are standing at the center of your living room facing the south wall; you have been here before; you know how much light enters this room during the day, and you recognize what is in front of you; (pause) what is behind you. (pause)

You know what is to your left, (pause) and what is to your right. (pause)

At the count of 3, we will change the scene to night time with the house lights turned on. 1—2—3 (snap fingers). The scene has changed to night time, and you are still standing in the middle of the living room, facing the south wall. You have been here before, and you know what is in front of you, (pause) what is behind you, (pause) what is to your left, (pause) and what is to your right. (pause)

At the count of 3, the lights will go out. 1—2—3 (snap fingers). The lights are out and you are standing in darkness facing the south wall. Although the living room looks dark, you still know what is in front of you, (pause) what is behind you, (pause) what is to your left, (pause) and what is to your right. (pause)

At this time concentrate on the wall before you, the south wall. You can sense it being a certain distance away and you know what is on this wall; you also know the color of this wall. Use your memory, your knowing, your sensing, to make a study of the south wall.

Scan this wall as you did the front of your home, beginning at the upper left corner and going from left to right, a little lower each time until you reach the floor level. Study everything that attracts you: Pictures, curtains, and furniture. Especially concentrate on objects that contain color.

(**Instructor**: Allow about 1 minute for this, occasionally saying, "Take your time," "study colors.")

Now mentally walk toward the south wall and stand close enough to touch it. (pause) At the count of 3 you will objectively raise your hand to touch the wall. 1—2—3 (snap fingers).

Objectively stretch out your arm, raise your hand and with the palm of your hand touch the wall. Use your imagination to sense the wall as being smooth or rough, (pause) as cold or warm. (pause) Whatever you perceive with your imagination at this dimension you can use as a point of reference in the future.

Subjectively observe and study the wall from a few inches away. Study the material, (pause) the color. (pause) Whatever you perceive with your imagination at this dimension you can use as a point of reference in the future.

At the count of 3 you will imagine projecting yourself subjectively within the wall. 1—2—3 (snap fingers). You are now within the wall. You may return your hand to rest on your lap. At this time, we will conduct four tests subjectively. First we will test for light, intensity and color; our second test is for temperature; the third test is for odor; and the fourth, for solidity of material by reflected sound.

At the count of 3, we will test for light, its intensity and color. 1—2—3 (snap fingers). Subjectively test for light, intensity and color; how much light do you sense? (pause) What color do you sense? (pause) Whatever you perceive with your imagination at this dimension you can use as a point of reference in the future.

At the count of 3, test for temperature. 1—2—3 (snap fingers). Subjectively test for temperature. (pause) Is there a difference in temperature between the inside and the outside of the wall? (pause) Whatever you perceive with your imagination at this dimension you can use as a point of reference in the future.

At the count of 3, test for odor. 1—2—3 (snap fingers). Subjectively test for odor. (pause) Is there a difference in odor between the inside and outside of the wall? (pause) Whatever you perceive with your imagination at this dimension you can use as a point of reference in the future.

At the count of 3, test for solidity of material by knocking on the inside of the wall. 1—2—3 (snap fingers). Objectively form a fist and knock on the inside of the subjective wall; objectively go through the motions as you do when you knock on a door. (pause) What kind of sound would you expect to hear reflected back to you? (pause) How solid would you judge the material to be? (pause) Whatever you perceive with your imagination at this dimension you can use as a point of reference in the future.

At the count of 3, you will come out of the wall and be just a few inches away from it. 1—2—3 (snap fingers). You are out of the wall, just a few inches away. Now at the count of 3 you will be at arm's length. 1—2—3 (snap fingers). You are now at arm's length.

At the count of 3 you will be at the center of your living room facing the south wall. 1—2—3 (snap fingers). You are now at the center of your living room, facing the south wall.

You know the color of your living room wall. At the count of 3, the color of the wall will change to black. 1—2—3 (snap fingers). The color of the wall is now black. (pause) You can get a true black color by imagining a painter with a can of black paint and a brush in his hand, painting the wall black and about to finish painting it. (pause)

The south wall is now all black. At the count of 3 it will be red. 1—2—3 (snap fingers). It is now red. (pause) To get a true red color, again imagine the painter about to finish painting it red. (pause) At the count of 3, the wall will be green. 1—2—3 (snap fingers). The wall is now green; (pause) imagine it green. (pause) At the count of 3 the wall will be blue. 1—2—3 (snap fingers). The wall is now blue; (pause) imagine it blue. (pause) At the count of 3 the wall will be violet. 1—2—3 (snap fingers). The wall is now violet; (pause) imagine it violet. (pause) We will change the color back to blue (snap fingers), back to green (snap fingers), back to red (snap fingers), back to black (snap fingers).

We will now mentally examine a chair, selecting any chair we wish. (pause) Mentally push it against the black wall. From your position in the center of the living room facing the south wall, mentally lift the chair about 20 degrees above the horizontal plane of sight, in the area of your Mental Screen. (pause)

We will examine the chair, studying its material, (pause) the upholstery, if it is upholstered, and how it is attached to the chair, (pause) and the color of the chair. (pause)

Now mentally turn the chair toward the left, (pause) now away from you, (pause) now toward the right, (pause) now facing you. (pause) Whatever you perceive with your imagination at this dimension you can use as a point of reference in the future.

At the count of 3, the color of the wall will change to its actual color. 1—2—3 (snap fingers). The wall is now its actual color; again study the chair; how does it stand out against this background? (pause) Whatever you perceive with your imagination at this dimension you can use as a point of reference in the future.

At the count of 3, the color of the wall will change to red. 1—2—3 (snap fingers). The wall is now red; study the chair; how does it stand out against a red background? (pause) Whatever you perceive with your imagination at this dimension you can use as a point of reference in the future.

At the count of 3, the color of the wall will change to green. 1—2—3 (snap fingers). The wall is now green; study the chair; how does it stand out against a green background? (pause) Whatever you perceive with your imagination at this dimension you can use as a point of reference in the future.

At the count of 3, the color of the wall will change to blue. 1—2—3 (snap fingers). The wall is now blue; study the chair; how does it stand out against a blue background? (pause) Whatever you perceive with your imagination at this dimension you can use as a point of reference in the future. The color of the wall will now change back to green (snap fingers), back to red (snap fingers), back to the natural color (snap fingers), back to black (snap fingers). At the count of 3, the chair will disappear from the scene. 1—2—3 (snap fingers). The chair has disappeared from the scene.

The wall is now black; at the count of 3, we will mentally bring into the scene a watermelon. It will be up against the wall at the height where we had the chair. 1—2—3 (snap fingers). Study this watermelon; use your knowing, your memory, your sensing; above all, use your imagination to study the watermelon. (pause) Observe how the green stands out against the black background. (pause)

At the count of 3, the watermelon will be cut in half. 1—2—3 (snap fingers). The watermelon is now cut in half, and you can visualize how the red portion of the watermelon, lined with black seeds, stands out against the white inner rind and the green of the outside. (pause) As you mentally bring the two halves slowly toward you, notice how they appear to increase in size; examine the various colors: The red, the white, the black, and the green from only a few inches away. (pause) Now imagine the odor and taste of watermelon. (pause) Whatever you perceive with your imagination at this dimension you can use as a point of reference in the future.

At the count of 3, the watermelon will be near the wall. 1—2—3 (snap fingers). The watermelon is now near the wall. At the count of 3, the two halves will come together. 1—2—3 (snap fingers). Now at the count of 3, the watermelon will disappear from the scene. 1—2—3 (snap fingers). The watermelon has disappeared from the scene.

At the count of 3, a lemon will appear at the same level, near the wall. 1—2—3 (snap fingers). A lemon appears in a fluorescent yellow color that stands out against the black wall. (pause) Bring the lemon closer to you, noticing how it appears to increase in size as it approaches; stop the approaching lemon when it is only a few inches away and examine its color. (pause) Now imagine the odor and taste of a lemon. (pause) Whatever you perceive with your imagination at this dimension you can use as a point of reference in the future.

At the count of 3, the lemon will be near the wall. 1—2—3 (snap fingers). The lemon is now near the wall, a little higher than the horizontal level of sight. At the count of 3, the lemon will disappear from the scene. 1—2—3 (snap fingers). The lemon has disappeared from the scene.

At the count of 3, an orange will appear. 1—2—3 (snap fingers). An orange has appeared on the scene; observe the color at a distance. (pause) Now bring the orange closer; again observe the color. (pause) Now imagine the odor and taste of an orange. (pause) Whatever you perceive with your imagination at this dimension you can use as a point of reference in the future.

At the count of 3, the orange will be near the wall. 1—2—3 (snap fingers). The orange is now near the wall. At the count of 3, the orange will disappear from the scene. 1—2—3 (snap fingers). The orange has disappeared from the scene.

At the count of 3, three bananas will appear. 1—2—3 (snap fingers). Three bananas have appeared; study the color from far and near. (pause) Now imagine the odor and taste of bananas. (pause) Whatever you perceive with your imagination at this dimension you can use as a point of reference in the future.

At the count of 3, the bananas will be near the wall. 1—2—3 (snap fingers). Now at the count of 3, the bananas will disappear from the scene. 1—2—3 (snap fingers). The bananas have disappeared from the scene.

At the count of 3, three carrots will appear. 1—2—3 (snap fingers). Three carrots have appeared; study the color from far and near. (pause) Now imagine the odor and taste of carrots. (pause) Whatever you perceive with your imagination at this dimension you can use as a point of reference in the future.

At the count of 3, the carrots will be near the wall. 1—2—3 (snap fingers). Now at the count of 3, the carrots will disappear from the scene. 1—2—3 (snap fingers). The carrots have disappeared from the scene.

At the count of 3, a fresh and crisp head of lettuce will appear. 1—2—3 (snap fingers). A head of lettuce has appeared; study the color from far. (pause) Now bring it closer and study the color from a distance of about 12 inches. (pause) Whatever you perceive with your imagination at this dimension you can use as a point of reference in the future.

At the count of 3, the head of lettuce will be near the wall. 1—2—3 (snap fingers). Now at the count of 3, the head of lettuce will disappear from the scene. 1—2—3 (snap fingers). The head of lettuce has disappeared from the scene. Whatever you perceive with your imagination at this dimension, you can use as points of reference in the future. It is now an accomplished fact that subjective points of reference have been established at the imaginative dimension, at the subjective dimension, at different levels and different depths. To function at these levels and to use these points of reference, all you need is to have a sincere desire to solve problems.

IMPRESSION OF NEW MATERIAL—PROGRAMMING THE 3-SCENES TECHNIQUE

We will now impress and program the 3-Scenes Technique, a technique that you can use to help you implement your decisions and the guidance that you receive.

When you desire to use the 3-Scenes Technique, go to your center with the 3 to 1 method.

Create and project onto your Mental Screen, directly in front of you, using visualization, an image of the existing situation.

Recall details of what the situation looks like in this first scene. Make a good study of the existing situation so you are completely aware of all aspects of it.

If you have programmed for this project previously, then take into account any changes that have taken place since your most recent programming session.

After making a good study of the existing situation, then shift your awareness to your left, approximately 15 degrees. In a second scene, to the left of the first scene, use imagination to mentally picture yourself taking action and doing something to implement your decisions, and to follow the guidance you have received, and imagine the desired changes beginning to take place.

Now in a third scene, another 15 degrees farther to your left, use your imagination to create and project an image of the situation the way you desire for it to end up. Imagine many people benefiting. The more people who benefit, the better.

Anytime in the future when you think of this project, visualize (recall) the image that you created of the desired end result in the third scene.

PROGRAMMING THE MENTALVIDEO TECHNIQUE

Programming a technique, the MentalVideo Technique that you can use for problem solving.

Whenever you need to solve a problem, make a decision, or obtain guidance with the MentalVideo Technique, proceed in the following manner:

At beta, with your eyes open, mentally create, with visualization, a MentalVideo of a problem, or the existing situation. Include everything that belongs to the animate matter kingdom. Animate matter means everything that contains life.

After you have completed the MentalVideo of the problem, use visualization to review it at beta, with your eyes closed.

Later, when you are in bed and ready to go to sleep, go to your center with the 3 to 1 method. Once you are at your center, review the MentalVideo that you created of the problem, or the existing situation, when you were at the beta level.

After you have reviewed the problem, mentally convert the problem into a project. Then create, with imagination, a MentalVideo of the solution.

The MentalVideo of the solution should contain a step-by-step procedure of how you desire the project to be resolved.

After both of the MentalVideos have been completed, go to sleep with the intention of delivering the MentalVideos to your tutor while you sleep. Take for granted that the delivery will be made.

During the next three days, look for indications that point to the solution. Every time you think of the project, think of the solution that you created in the MentalVideo, in a past tense sense.

POST EFFECTS—PREVIEW OF NEXT SESSION

You have practiced entering deep, healthy levels of mind. In your next session, you will enter a deeper, healthier level of mind, faster and easier than this time.

POST EFFECTS—SPECIAL

Every time you function at these levels of the mind and at these points of reference, you will receive beneficial effects physically and mentally.

You may use these levels of the mind and these points of reference to help yourself physically and mentally.

You may use these levels of the mind and these points of reference to help your loved ones, physically and mentally.

You may use these levels of the mind and these points of reference to help any human being who needs help, physically and mentally.

You will never use these levels of the mind or these points of reference to harm any human being; if this be your intention, you will not be able to function within these levels of the mind, nor will you be able to use these points of reference.

You will always use these levels of the mind and these points of reference in a constructive, creative manner for all that is good, honest, pure, clean, and positive. And this is so.

(**Instructor**: Read the following paragraph only during the last conditioning cycle of the day.)

You will continue to strive to take part in constructive and creative activities to make this a better world to live in, so that when we move on, we shall have left behind a better world for those who follow. You will consider the whole of humanity, depending on their ages, as fathers or mothers, brothers or sisters, sons or daughters. You are a superior human being; you have greater understanding, compassion, and patience with others.

BRING OUT

In a moment, I am going to count from 1 to 5 and cause a sound with my fingers. At that moment, you will open your eyes, be wide awake, feeling fine and in perfect health, feeling better than before. You will have no ill effects whatsoever in your head, no headache; no ill effects whatsoever in your hearing, no buzzing in your ears; no ill effects whatsoever in your vision and eyesight; vision, eyesight, and hearing improve every time you function at these levels of mind.

1—2—coming out slowly now.

3—at the count of 5, you will open your eyes, be wide awake, feeling fine and in perfect health, feeling better than before, feeling the way you feel when you have slept the right amount of revitalizing, refreshing, relaxing, healthy, wonderful sleep.

4—5 (snap fingers) eyes open, wide awake, feeling fine and in perfect health, feeling better than before.

THIS CONCLUDES THE PROJECTION TO HOME EXERCISE FOR JOSÉ SILVA'S ULTRAMIND ESP SYSTEMS.

CHAPTER 16

Mental Projection into Metals

Prerequisite: Projection to Home Exercise

José Silva advised practicing the Centering Exercise prior to each of the five mental projection exercises.

Please read through the "Impression of New Material" first, before you go to your level, so you will know what to expect. This is known as "preconditioning."

Remember to handle the four metals and establish objective points of reference before you begin.

Perhaps you have stainless steel cookware or cooking utensils you can use, a copper pot or copper tubing, a brass belt buckle or bell or other brass item, and aluminum cans or other items. If not, you can purchase them at any hardware store.

The idea is: You already have experience using your physical senses to identify the item—you know what steel looks like (sight), what it feels like (touch), the sound it makes when you tap on it (hearing), and what it smells like. Steel sure doesn't smell like the old brass French horn I used to play.

Now you are going to handle the object—look at it, feel it, smell it, listen to the sound when you tap on it—and then enter your level and project yourself mentally into the object, and then use your mind—your psychic senses—and establish points of reference so you can identify it in the future with your psychic senses.

If nothing comes to you, just make it up. It is your way of identifying and differentiating between the items. Just follow the instructions.

Then you will do the same with leaves, and you will have all of the building blocks for physical matter, and then you can easily learn to detect any information you need about anybody and anything, if you need that information to solve a problem.

Allow yourself enough time to complete the entire exercise, about 37 minutes. Turn off all communications devices and ask people not to disturb you so you can go through the entire exercise uninterrupted.

Here is the complete Projection into Metals exercise:

MENTAL VIDEO PRACTICE SESSION

Let us, at beta with eyes open, mentally create, with visualization, a MentalVideo of a problem or a situation concerning health.

Include everything that belongs to the animate matter kingdom. Animate matter means everything that contains life. The MentalVideo must include everything animate that concerns the problem.

After having completed the MentalVideo of the problem, use visualization to review it at beta, with your eyes closed.

Mental Projection into Metals

DEEPENING (physical relaxation at level 3)

We will start this exercise with the 3 to 1 method.

Find a comfortable position, close your eyes, take a deep breath, and, while exhaling, mentally repeat and visualize the number 3 three times. (pause)

To help you learn to relax physically at level 3, I am going to direct your attention to different parts of your body.

(**Instructor**: Pause after every mention.)

Relax your scalp; relax your forehead; relax your eyes; relax your face; relax your throat; relax your shoulders; relax your chest externally and internally; relax your abdominal area externally and internally; relax your thighs; relax your knees; relax your calves; relax your feet.

You are now at a deeper, healthier level of mind, deeper than before.

This is your physical relaxation level 3. Whenever you mentally repeat and visualize the number 3, your body will relax as completely as you are now, and more so every time you practice.

DEEPENING (mental relaxation at level 2)

To enter mental relaxation level 2, take a deep breath and while exhaling mentally repeat and visualize the number 2 three times, and you are at level 2, a deeper level than 3. (pause) Level 2 is for mental relaxation, where noises will not distract you. Instead, noises will help you to relax mentally more and more.

To improve mental relaxation at level 2, practice visualizing tranquil and passive scenes. (pause)

TO ENTER YOUR CENTER

Take another deep breath and while exhaling, mentally repeat and visualize number 1 three times. (pause)

You are now at level 1, a deeper, healthier level of mind where you can function from your center.

DEEPENING (routine cycle)

To help you enter a deeper, healthier level of mind, I am going to count from 10 to 1. On each descending number, you will feel yourself going deeper and you will enter a deeper, healthier level of mind.

10—9—feel going deeper,

8—7—6—deeper and deeper,

5—4—3—deeper and deeper,

2—1

You are now at a deeper, healthier level of mind, deeper than before.

It is a wonderful feeling to be deeply relaxed, a very healthy state of being.

EFFECTIVE SENSORY PROJECTION STATEMENTS

Effective Sensory Projection statements for success.

I am now learning to attune my intelligence by developing my sensing faculties and to project them to any point or place on this planet so as to be aware of any actions taking place, if this is necessary and beneficial for humanity.

I am now learning to attune my intelligence by developing my sensing faculties and to project them to any point or place on any planet within the solar system, any solar system within the galaxy, and any galaxy within the universe so as to be aware of any actions taking place, if this is necessary and beneficial for humanity.

I am now learning to attune my intelligence by developing my sensing faculties and to project them to the different matter kingdoms: the inanimate matter kingdom, any of its levels and depths; the animate matter kingdom with reproductive intelligence, plant life and animal life, any of its levels and depths; and the animate matter kingdom with reproductive intelligence and an awareness of existence, the human body and mind kingdom, any of its levels and depths.

I am now learning to detect abnormalities whenever such abnormalities exist within any kingdom, any level, and any depth, if this is necessary and beneficial for humanity.

I am now learning to apply corrective measures and to bring back to normalcy any abnormality found within any kingdom, any level, and any depth, if this is necessary and beneficial for humanity.

Negative thoughts and negative suggestions have no influence over me at any level of the mind.

LAWS OF PROGRAMMING

The following laws are to be considered when programming:

You should do to others only what you like others to do to you.

The solution must help to make this planet a better place to live.

It must be the best for everybody concerned.

It must help at least two or more persons.

It must be within the possibility area.

PRINCIPLES TO KEEP IN MIND WHEN PROGRAMMING

The following principles apply to programming.

Objective physical communication takes place at the beta, left brain dimension using the objective—physical—senses. The hearing is used for perception, and the voice is used for transmission.

Subjective—mental—communication takes place at your center, the alpha, right brain dimension by using the subjective senses. Visualization is used for perception, and imagination is used for transmission.

In the objective—physical—dimension, the past is behind us, the present is our present position, and the future is ahead of us.

In the subjective—mental—dimension, the past is to your right, the present is centered straight ahead, and the future is to your left.

IMPRESSION OF NEW MATERIAL (programming)

We will now program Effective Sensory Projection for your success, and program information with the use of mental projection for your benefit. We will establish subjective points of reference at the inanimate matter kingdom, at different levels and depths for stainless steel, copper, brass, and aluminum.

In a moment I am going to count from 1 to 3 and cause a sound with my fingers; at that time you will project yourself mentally to the living room in your home and imagine yourself standing in the center, facing the south wall. 1—2—3 (snap fingers). You are now standing in the center of your living room facing the south wall.

At the count of 3, you will extend your arm objectively and visualize the piece of stainless steel. 1—2—3 (snap fingers). Extend your arm objectively and visualize the piece of stainless steel; mentally sense the piece of stainless steel and relive and objectively repeat all the movements made previously. (pause) Bring it closer and closer to your forehead; mentally observe the steel a few inches away. (pause)

Now allow it to touch your forehead, and mentally project yourself into the stainless steel. (pause) You are now within the piece of stainless steel. You may return your hand to rest on your lap. If you imagine the piece of stainless steel to be just big enough for you to fit in it, then you will not go very deeply inside; but if you imagine the piece of steel as big as this room, then you can go further within. If you will imagine this piece of steel to be as large as a massive building, and feel your size in contrast with it, then you can go still further within, using the depth that this dimension of mind offers.

Whenever you need to increase the illumination or amount or size of anything, just snap the fingers of your right hand slightly, and expect the change to take place. For a decrease, or to return anything back to its original state, snap the fingers of your left hand slightly, and expect the change to take place. Whatever you perceive with your imagination at this dimension, you can use as points of reference in the future.

At this time we are going to subjectively conduct four tests. The first test will be for light, intensity and color. 1—2—3 (snap fingers). Sense the intensity and color of light within the stainless steel. (pause) Whatever you perceive with your imagination at this dimension, you can use as a point of reference in the future.

At the count of 3, we will test for temperature. 1—2—3 (snap fingers). Sense the temperature within the stainless steel. (pause) Whatever you perceive with your imagination at this dimension, you can use as a point of reference in the future.

At the count of 3, we will test for odor. 1—2—3 (snap fingers). Sense the odor within the stainless steel. (pause) Whatever you perceive with your imagination at this dimension, you can use as a point of reference in the future.

At the count of 3, we will test for solidity of material by knocking on the stainless steel. 1—2—3 (snap fingers). Objectively form a fist and go through the motions of knocking on the stainless steel as you do on a wall. (pause) What kind of sound do you subjectively hear? (pause) Whatever you perceive with your imagination at this dimension, you can use as a point of reference in the future.

At the count of 3, you will objectively touch your forehead. 1—2—3 (snap fingers). Touch your forehead; you are now coming out of the stainless steel. Objectively extend your arm and allow the imaginary piece of steel to float in space by itself, at a level a little higher than the horizontal plane, or level, of sight. You may return your hand to rest on your lap.

How does the piece of stainless steel stand out against the natural color of the wall? Keep the piece of stainless steel rotating in your imagination; keep it moving; keep it dynamic. (pause)

At the count of 3, the color of the wall will change to red. 1—2—3 (snap fingers). The wall is now red. Keep the piece of steel rotating, noticing how it stands out against the red background. (pause)

At the count of 3, the color of the wall will change to green. 1—2—3 (snap fingers). The wall is now green. Notice how the piece of rotating steel stands out against the green background. (pause)

At the count of 3, the color of the wall will change to blue. 1—2—3 (snap fingers). The wall is now blue. Notice how the piece of rotating steel stands out against the blue background. (pause)

The color of the wall will now change back to green (snap fingers), back to red (snap fingers), back to the actual color of the wall (snap fingers). Now the piece of stainless steel will disappear from the scene. (snap fingers). The piece of stainless steel has disappeared from the scene.

At the count of 3, we will play back the impressions made with copper. 1—2—3 (snap fingers). Extend your arm objectively and mentally play back the previous impressions made with copper; repeat every movement; bring your hand closer and closer. (pause)

Now touch your forehead, and mentally project yourself into the piece of copper. (pause) In your imagination you are now within the piece of copper, any depth of this level you desire. You may return your hand to rest on your lap. Remember to use your finger-snapping controls to increase and decrease as necessary.

At the count of 3, we will conduct the first test. 1—2—3 (snap fingers). Sense the intensity and color of light within copper. (pause) How does the light within copper compare with that of stainless steel? (pause) Whatever you perceive with your imagination at this dimension, you can use as a point of reference in the future.

At the count of 3, test for temperature. 1—2—3 (snap fingers). Sense the temperature within copper. (pause) How does the temperature of copper compare with that of stainless steel? (pause) Whatever you perceive with your imagination at this dimension, you can use as a point of reference in the future.

At the count of 3, test for odor. 1—2—3 (snap fingers). Sense the odor within copper. (pause) How does the odor of copper compare with that of stainless steel? (pause) Whatever you perceive with your imagination at this dimension, you can use as a point of reference in the future.

At the count of 3, test for solidity of material. 1—2—3 (snap fingers). Objectively form a fist and knock on copper. (pause) How does the imagined sound of copper compare with that of stainless steel? (pause) Whatever you perceive with your imagination at this dimension, you can use as a point of reference in the future.

At the count of 3, touch your forehead to come out of the piece of copper. 1—2—3 (snap fingers). Touch your forehead; you are now coming out of the copper. Extend your arm and hold the piece of copper at arm's length. Now allow the piece of copper to float in space using as a background the natural color of your living room south wall. Keep the piece of copper rotating. You may return your hand to rest on your lap. (pause)

At the count of 3, the color of the wall will change to red. 1—2—3 (snap fingers). The wall is now red. How does this piece of copper stand out against a red background? (pause) How does this compare with the piece of stainless steel? Keep the piece of copper rotating. (pause)

At the count of 3, the color of the wall will change to green. 1—2—3 (snap fingers). The wall is now green. How does this piece of copper stand out against a green background? (pause) How does this compare with the stainless steel? Keep the piece of copper rotating. (pause)

At the count of 3, the color of the wall will change to blue. 1—2—3 (snap fingers). The wall is now blue. How does this piece of copper stand out against a blue background? (pause) How does this compare with the stainless steel? Keep the piece of copper rotating. (pause)

The color of the wall will now change back to green (snap fingers), back to red (snap fingers), back to the actual color of the wall (snap fingers). Now the piece of copper will disappear from the scene (snap fingers). The piece of copper has disappeared from the scene.

At the count of 3, we will visualize the piece of brass. 1—2—3 (snap fingers). Extend your arm objectively and visualize the piece of brass, reliving all your previous movements as you bring your hand closer and closer. (pause) Now touch your forehead, and mentally project yourself into the brass. (pause) You are now within the brass at any depth or level you desire. You may return your hand to rest on your lap.

At the count of 3, we will conduct the first test. 1—2—3 (snap fingers). Sense the intensity and color of light within brass. (pause) How does the light within brass compare with that of copper, (pause) and stainless steel? (pause) Whatever you perceive with your imagination at this dimension, you can use as a point of reference in the future.

At the count of 3, test for temperature. 1—2—3 (snap fingers). Sense the temperature within brass. (pause) How does the temperature of brass compare with that of copper, (pause) and stainless steel? (pause) Whatever you perceive with your imagination at this dimension, you can use as a point of reference in the future.

At the count of 3, test for odor. 1—2—3 (snap fingers). Sense the odor within brass. (pause) How does the odor of brass compare with that of copper, (pause) and stainless steel? (pause) Whatever you perceive with your imagination at this dimension, you can use as a point of reference in the future.

At the count of 3, test for solidity of material. 1—2—3 (snap fingers). Objectively form a fist and knock on brass. (pause) How does the reflected sound of brass compare with that of copper, (pause) and stainless steel? (pause) Whatever you perceive with your imagination at this dimension, you can use as a point of reference in the future.

At the count of 3, touch your forehead to come out of the piece of brass. 1—2—3 (snap fingers). Touch your forehead; you are now coming out of the brass. Extend your arm and hold the piece of brass at arm's length. Now allow the piece of brass to float in space using as a background the natural color of your living room south wall. Keep the piece of brass rotating. You may return your hand to rest on your lap. (pause)

At the count of 3, the color of the wall will change to red. 1—2—3 (snap fingers). The wall is now red. How does this piece of brass stand out against a red background? (pause) How does this compare with the piece of copper, (pause) and stainless steel? Keep the piece of brass rotating. (pause)

At the count of 3, the color of the wall will change to green. 1—2—3 (snap fingers). The wall is now green. How does this piece of brass stand out against a green background? (pause) How does this compare with the copper, (pause) and stainless steel? Keep the piece of brass rotating. (pause)

At the count of 3, the color of the wall will change to blue. 1—2—3 (snap fingers). The wall is now blue. How does this piece of brass stand out against a blue background? (pause) How does this compare with the copper, (pause) and stainless steel? Keep the piece of brass rotating. (pause)

The color of the wall will now change back to green (snap fingers), back to red (snap fingers), back to the actual color of the wall (snap fingers). Now the piece of brass will disappear from the scene (snap fingers). The piece of brass has disappeared from the scene.

At the count of 3, we will visualize the piece of aluminum. 1—2—3 (snap fingers).

Extend your arm objectively and visualize the piece of aluminum, reliving all your previous movements, bringing your hand closer and closer. (pause) Now touch your forehead and mentally project yourself into the piece of aluminum. (pause) You are now within the piece of aluminum, at any depth or level you desire. You may return your hand to rest on your lap.

At the count of 3, we will conduct the first test. 1—2—3 (snap fingers). Sense the intensity and color of light within aluminum. (pause) How does the light within aluminum compare with that of brass, (pause) copper, (pause) and stainless steel? (pause)

Whatever you perceive with your imagination at this dimension, you can use as a point of reference in the future.

At the count of 3, test for temperature. 1—2—3 (snap fingers). Sense the temperature within aluminum. (pause) How does the temperature of aluminum compare with that of brass, (pause) copper, (pause) and stainless steel? (pause) Whatever you perceive with your imagination at this dimension, you can use as a point of reference in the future.

At the count of 3, test for odor. 1—2—3 (snap fingers). Sense the odor within aluminum. (pause) How does the odor of aluminum compare with that of brass, (pause) copper, (pause) and stainless steel? (pause) Whatever you perceive with your imagination at this dimension, you can use as a point of reference in the future.

At the count of 3, test for solidity of material. 1—2—3 (snap fingers). Objectively form a fist and knock on aluminum. (pause) How does the reflected sound of aluminum compare with that of brass, (pause) copper, (pause) and stainless steel? (pause) Whatever you perceive with your imagination at this dimension, you can use as a point of reference in the future.

At the count of 3, touch your forehead to come out of the piece of aluminum. 1—2—3 (snap fingers). Touch your forehead; you are now coming out of the aluminum. Extend your arm and hold the piece of aluminum at arm's length. Now allow the piece of aluminum to float in space using as a background the natural color of your living room south wall. Keep the piece of aluminum rotating. You may return your hand to rest on your lap. (pause)

At the count of 3, the color of the wall will change to red. 1—2—3 (snap fingers). The wall is now red. How does the piece of aluminum stand out against a red background? (pause) How does this compare with the piece of brass, (pause) copper, (pause) and stainless steel? Keep the piece of aluminum rotating. (pause)

At the count of 3, the color of the wall will change to green. 1—2—3 (snap fingers). The wall is now green. How does this piece of aluminum stand out against a green background? (pause) How does this compare with brass, (pause) copper, (pause) and stainless steel? Keep the piece of aluminum rotating. (pause)

At the count of 3, the color of the wall will change to blue. 1—2—3 (snap fingers). The wall is now blue. How does this piece of aluminum stand out against a blue background? (pause) How does this compare with the brass, (pause) copper, (pause) and stainless steel? Keep the piece of aluminum rotating. (pause)

The color of the wall will now change back to green (snap fingers), back to red (snap fingers), back to the actual color of the wall (snap fingers). Now the piece of aluminum will disappear from the scene (snap fingers). The piece of aluminum has disappeared from the scene.

Whatever you perceive with your imagination at this dimension, you can use as points of reference in the future. It is now an accomplished fact that subjective points of reference have been established at the inanimate matter kingdom at different levels and different depths. To function at these levels and to use these points of reference, all you need is to have a sincere desire to solve problems. Your mind will automatically seek out these points of reference where you will perceive and become aware of information you can use to solve such problems. And this is so.

PROGRAM HOW TO USE PSYCHOMETRY

We will now impress information for your benefit: How to use psychometry, a technique that you can use to detect information.

First, select an object that has been in the possession of the person about whom you desire to detect information, and hold this object in your left hand.

Then enter your level with the 3 to 1 method. Once at your level, determine what information you are seeking. For instance, is the information that you desire physical, mental, or emotional?

Relax and start thinking about the person who previously had this object in their possession. You may ask any kind of question you desire about this person; then clear your mind for a moment of time, and start thinking again to detect the answer.

When you have a sincere desire to detect this information, because you need it to improve conditions on the planet in some manner, your mind will automatically adjust to the specific level where you will be accurate and correct.

PROGRAM MENTALVIDEO FOR HEALTH

Programming a technique, the MentalVideo Technique that you can use for problem solving.

Whenever you need to solve a problem with the MentalVideo Technique, enter level 1 with the 3 to 1 method when you are in bed and ready to go to sleep. Once you are at your level, review the MentalVideo that you created of the problem previously when you were at beta.

After you have reviewed the problem, mentally convert the problem into a project. Then create, with imagination, a MentalVideo of the solution.

The MentalVideo of the solution should contain a step-by-step procedure of how you desire the project to be resolved.

After both of the MentalVideos have been completed, go to sleep with the intention of delivering the MentalVideos to your tutor while you sleep. Take for granted that the delivery will be made.

During the next three days, look for indications that point to the solution. Every time you think of the project, think of the solution that you created in the MentalVideo, in a past tense sense.

POST EFFECTS—PREVIEW OF NEXT SESSION

You have practiced entering deep, healthy levels of mind. In your next session, you will enter a deeper, healthier level of mind, faster and easier than this time.

POST EFFECTS—SPECIAL

Every time you function at these levels of the mind and at these points of reference, you will receive beneficial effects physically and mentally.

You may use these levels of the mind and these points of reference to help yourself physically and mentally.

You may use these levels of the mind and these points of reference to help your loved ones, physically and mentally.

You may use these levels of the mind and these points of reference to help any human being who needs help, physically and mentally.

You will never use these levels of the mind or these points of reference to harm any human being; if this be your intention, you will not be able to function within these levels of the mind, nor will you be able to use these points of reference.

You will always use these levels of the mind and these points of reference in a constructive, creative manner for all that is good, honest, pure, clean, and positive. And this is so.

You will continue to strive to take part in constructive and creative activities to make this a better world to live in, so that when we move on, we shall have left behind a better world for those who follow. You will consider the whole of humanity, depending on their ages, as fathers or mothers, brothers or sisters, sons or daughters. You are a superior human being; you have greater understanding, compassion, and patience with others.

BRING OUT

In a moment, I am going to count from 1 to 5 and cause a sound with my fingers. At that moment, you will open your eyes, be wide awake, feeling fine and in perfect health, feeling better than before. You will have no ill effects whatsoever in your head, no headache; no ill effects whatsoever in your hearing, no buzzing in your ears; no ill effects whatsoever in your vision and eyesight; vision, eyesight, and hearing improve every time you function at these levels of mind.

1—2—coming out slowly now.

3—at the count of 5, you will open your eyes, be wide awake, feeling fine and in perfect health, feeling better than before, feeling the way you feel when you have slept the right amount of revitalizing, refreshing, relaxing, healthy, wonderful sleep.

4—5 (snap fingers) eyes open, wide awake, feeling fine and in perfect health, feeling better than before.

THIS CONCLUDES THE PROJECTION INTO METALS EXERCISE FOR JOSÉ SILVA'S ULTRAMIND ESP SYSTEMS.

CHAPTER 17

Mental Projection into Plant Life

Prerequisite: Projection into Metals Exercise

José Silva advised practicing the Centering Exercise prior to each of the five mental projection exercises.

Please read through the "Impression of New Material" first, before you go to your level, so you will know what to expect. This is known as "preconditioning."

Please get two leaves to use for this exercise, from two different species of plants.

Allow yourself enough time to complete the entire exercise, about 29 minutes. Turn off all communications devices and ask people not to disturb you so you can go through the entire exercise uninterrupted.

Here is the complete Projection to Tree and into Leaves exercise:

MENTAL VIDEO PRACTICE SESSION

Let us, at beta with eyes open, mentally create, with visualization, a MentalVideo of a problem or a situation concerning relationships.

Include everything that belongs to the animate matter kingdom. Animate matter means everything that contains life. The MentalVideo must include everything animate that concerns the problem.

After having completed the MentalVideo of the problem, use visualization to review it at beta, with your eyes closed.

Mental Projection to a Fruit Tree and into Leaves

DEEPENING (physical relaxation at level 3)
We will start this exercise with the 3 to 1 method.

Find a comfortable position, close your eyes, take a deep breath and while exhaling, mentally repeat and visualize the number 3 three times. (pause)

To help you learn to relax physically at level 3, I am going to direct your attention to different parts of your body.

(**Instructor**: Pause after every mention.)

Relax your scalp; relax your forehead; relax your eyes; relax your face; relax your throat; relax your shoulders; relax your chest externally and internally; relax your abdominal area externally and internally; relax your thighs; relax your knees; relax your calves; relax your feet.

You are now at a deeper, healthier level of mind, deeper than before. This is your physical relaxation level 3. Whenever you mentally repeat and visualize the number 3, your body will relax as completely as you are now, and more so every time you practice.

DEEPENING (mental relaxation at level 2)

To enter mental relaxation level 2, take a deep breath and while exhaling mentally repeat and visualize the number 2 three times, and you are at level 2, a deeper level than 3. (pause) Level 2 is for mental relaxation, where noises will not distract you. Instead, noises will help you to relax mentally more and more.

To improve mental relaxation at level 2, practice visualizing tranquil and passive scenes. (pause)

TO ENTER YOUR CENTER

Take another deep breath and while exhaling, mentally repeat and visualize number 1 three times. (pause)

You are now at level 1, a deeper, healthier level of mind where you can function from your center.

DEEPENING (routine cycle)

To help you enter a deeper, healthier level of mind, I am going to count from 10 to 1. On each descending number, you will feel yourself going deeper and you will enter a deeper, healthier level of mind.

10—9—feel going deeper,

8—7—6—deeper and deeper,

5—4—3—deeper and deeper,

2—1

You are now at a deeper, healthier level of mind, deeper than before. It is a wonderful feeling to be deeply relaxed, a very healthy state of being.

EFFECTIVE SENSORY PROJECTION STATEMENTS

Effective Sensory Projection statements for success.

I am now learning to attune my intelligence by developing my sensing faculties and to project them to any point or place on this planet so as to be aware of any actions taking place, if this is necessary and beneficial for humanity.

I am now learning to attune my intelligence by developing my sensing faculties and to project them to any point or place on any planet within the solar system, any solar system within the galaxy, and any galaxy within the universe so as to be aware of any actions taking place, if this is necessary and beneficial for humanity.

I am now learning to attune my intelligence by developing my sensing faculties and to project them to the different matter kingdoms: the inanimate matter kingdom, any of its levels and depths; the animate matter kingdom with reproductive intelligence, plant life and animal life, any of its levels and depths; and the animate matter kingdom with reproductive intelligence and an awareness of existence, the human body and mind kingdom, any of its levels and depths.

I am now learning to detect abnormalities whenever such abnormalities exist within any kingdom, any level, and any depth, if this is necessary and beneficial for humanity.

I am now learning to apply corrective measures and to bring back to normalcy any abnormality found within any kingdom, any level, and any depth, if this is necessary and beneficial for humanity.

Negative thoughts and negative suggestions have no influence over me at any level of the mind.

LAWS OF PROGRAMMING

The following laws are to be considered when programming:

You should do to others only what you like others to do to you.

The solution must help to make this planet a better place to live.

It must be the best for everybody concerned.

It must help at least two or more persons.

It must be within the possibility area.

PRINCIPLES TO KEEP IN MIND WHEN PROGRAMMING

The following principles apply to programming.

Objective physical communication takes place at the beta, left brain dimension using the objective—physical—senses. The hearing is used for perception, and the voice is used for transmission.

Subjective—mental—communication takes place at your center, the alpha, right brain dimension by using the subjective senses. Visualization is used for perception, and imagination is used for transmission.

In the objective—physical—dimension, the past is behind us, the present is our present position, and the future is ahead of us.

In the subjective—mental—dimension, the past is to your right, the present is centered straight ahead, and the future is to your left.

IMPRESSION OF NEW MATERIAL (programming)

We will now continue programming Effective Sensory Projection for your success, and program information with the use of mental projection for your benefit. We will establish subjective points of reference by projecting into the animate matter kingdom with reproductive intelligence, into the plant life kingdom, becoming aware of different levels and different depths. Our present project is projection to a fruit tree during seasonal changes, and a study of the leaves and fruit.

In a moment, I am going to count from 1 to 3 and cause a sound with my fingers; at that time you will project yourself mentally to be standing next to a fruit tree that blossoms before bearing fruit. 1—2—3 (snap fingers). You are now standing right next to a fruit tree that has only leaves.

At the count of 3, you will objectively extend your arm and reach out to cut off a leaf. 1—2—3 (snap fingers). Objectively extend your arm, reach out and cut off a leaf. (pause) Now mentally crush this leaf with your fingers; (pause) bring it to your nostrils, and mentally impress the odor. (pause) Whatever you perceive with your imagination at this dimension, you can use as a point of reference in the future.

Time is moving on; (pause) blossoms are beginning to appear; (pause) the tree is now in full bloom. At the count of 3, you will objectively reach out and cut off a blossom. 1—2—3 (snap fingers). Objectively reach out and cut off a blossom, (pause) crush it with your fingers, (pause) bring it to your nostrils, and mentally make an impression. (pause) Whatever you perceive with your imagination at this dimension, you can use as a point of reference in the future.

Time is moving on; (pause) blossoms are falling off; (pause) the tree now has very small unripened fruit. At the count of 3, you will reach out and cut off a small unripened fruit. 1—2—3 (snap fingers). Reach out and cut off a small unripened fruit;

(pause) crush it with your fingers; (pause) bring it to your nostrils, and mentally make an impression. (pause) Whatever you perceive with your imagination at this dimension, you can use as a point of reference in the future.

Time is moving on; (pause) the fruit is growing; (pause) it is now fully grown but unripened. At the count of 3, you will reach out and cut off a fully grown unripened fruit. 1—2—3 (snap fingers). Reach out and cut off a fully grown unripened fruit; (pause) break the skin; (pause) bring it to your nostrils, and mentally make an impression. (pause) Whatever you perceive with your imagination at this dimension, you can use as a point of reference in the future.

Time is moving on; (pause) the fruit is ripening; (pause) it is now ripe. At the count of 3, you will reach out and cut off a ripened fruit. 1—2—3 (snap fingers). Reach out and cut off a ripened fruit; (pause) break the skin; (pause) bring it to your nostrils, and mentally make an impression. (pause) Whatever you perceive with your imagination at this dimension, you can use as a point of reference in the future.

Now, at the count of 3, the tree will disappear and you will mentally project yourself to your living room. 1—2—3 (snap fingers). Mentally project yourself to the center of your living room, facing the south wall. You are now at the center of your living room, facing the south wall.

We will now replay the objective impressions of the leaves and also establish subjective points of reference. At the count of 3, we will visualize the first leaf. 1—2—3 (snap fingers). Extend your arm objectively and visualize the first leaf. Mentally sense the leaf. (pause) Bring it closer and closer to your forehead.

(pause) Now touch your forehead and mentally project yourself into the leaf. (pause) You are now within the first leaf. You may return your hand to rest on your lap.

At the count of 3, test for light. 1—2—3 (snap fingers). Sense the intensity and color of light within the leaf. (pause) How does light within the leaf compare with the light within aluminum, (pause) brass, (pause) copper, (pause) and stainless steel? (pause) Whatever you perceive with your imagination at this dimension, you can use as a point of reference in the future.

At the count of 3, test for temperature. 1—2—3 (snap fingers). Sense the temperature within the leaf. (pause) How does this compare with the temperature of aluminum, (pause) brass, (pause) copper, (pause) and stainless steel? (pause) Whatever you perceive with your imagination at this dimension, you can use as a point of reference in the future.

At the count of 3, test for odor. 1—2—3 (snap fingers). Sense the odor within the leaf. (pause) How does this compare with the odor of aluminum, (pause) brass, (pause) copper, (pause) and stainless steel? (pause) Whatever you perceive with your imagination at this dimension, you can use as a point of reference in the future.

At the count of 3, test for solidity of material. 1—2—3 (snap fingers). Objectively form a fist and knock on the inside of the leaf. (pause) How does this reflected sound compare with the reflected sound of aluminum, (pause) brass, (pause) copper, (pause) and stainless steel? (pause) Whatever you perceive with your imagination at this dimension, you can use as a point of reference in the future.

At the count of 3, touch your forehead to come out of the leaf. 1—2—3 (snap fingers). Touch your forehead; you are now coming out of the leaf. Extend your arm and mentally hold the leaf at arm's length. Now allow the leaf to float in space using the south wall of your living room as a background. Keep the leaf rotating. You may return your hand to rest on your lap. (pause)

At the count of 3, the color of the wall will change to red. 1—2—3 (snap fingers). How does the leaf stand out against a red background? (pause) How does this compare with aluminum, (pause) brass, (pause) copper, (pause) and stainless steel? (pause) Keep the leaf rotating. (pause)

At the count of 3, the color of the wall will change to green. 1—2—3 (snap fingers). How does the leaf stand out against a green background? (pause) How does this compare with aluminum, (pause) brass, (pause) copper, (pause) and stainless steel? (pause) Keep the leaf rotating.

At the count of 3, the color of the wall will change to blue. 1—2—3 (snap fingers). How does the leaf stand out against a blue background? (pause) How does this compare with aluminum, (pause) brass, (pause) copper, (pause) and stainless steel? (pause) Keep the leaf rotating.

The color of the wall will now change back to green (snap fingers), back to red (snap fingers), back to the actual color of the wall (snap fingers). Now the first leaf will disappear from the scene (snap fingers). The first leaf has disappeared from the scene.

At the count of 3, we will visualize the second leaf. 1—2—3 (snap fingers). Extend your arm objectively and visualize the second leaf. Mentally sense this leaf as you bring it closer and closer toward your forehead. (pause) Now touch your forehead and mentally project yourself into the leaf. (pause) You are now within the leaf. You may return your hand to rest on your lap.

At the count of 3, test for light. 1—2—3 (snap fingers). Sense the intensity and color of the light within this second leaf. (pause) How does the light within this leaf compare with the light within the first leaf? (pause) Whatever you perceive with your imagination at this dimension, you can use as a point of reference in the future.

At the count of 3, test for temperature. 1—2—3 (snap fingers). Sense the temperature within this leaf. (pause) How does it compare with the temperature within the first leaf? (pause) Whatever you perceive with your imagination at this dimension, you can use as a point of reference in the future.

At the count of 3, test for odor. 1—2—3 (snap fingers). Sense the odor within this same leaf. (pause) How does this compare with the odor of the other leaf? (pause) Whatever you perceive with your imagination at this dimension, you can use as a point of reference in the future.

At the count of 3, test for solidity of material. 1—2—3 (snap fingers). Objectively form a fist and knock on the inside of this second leaf. (pause) How does this sound compare with the sound of the first leaf? (pause) Whatever you perceive with your imagination at this dimension, you can use as a point of reference in the future.

At the count of 3, touch your forehead and come out of the leaf. 1—2—3 (snap fingers). Touch your forehead; you are now coming out of the leaf. Extend your arm and mentally hold the leaf at arm's length, allowing it to float in space against the background of your south wall. Keep the leaf rotating. You may return your hand to rest on your lap. (pause)

At the count of 3, the color of the wall will change to red. 1—2—3 (snap fingers). How does the second leaf stand out against a red background? (pause) How does this compare with the first leaf? Keep the second leaf rotating. (pause)

At the count of 3, the color of the wall will change to green. 1—2—3 (snap fingers). How does the leaf stand out against a green background? (pause) How does this compare with the first leaf? Keep the second leaf rotating. (pause)

At the count of 3, the color of the wall will change to blue. 1—2—3 (snap fingers). How does the leaf stand out against a blue background? (pause) How does this compare with the first leaf? Keep the second leaf rotating. (pause) The color of the wall will now change back to green (snap fingers), back to red (snap fingers), back to the actual color of the wall (snap fingers). The second leaf will now disappear from the scene (snap fingers). The second leaf has now disappeared.

Whatever you perceive with your imagination at this dimension, you can use as points of reference in the future. It is now an accomplished fact that subjective points of reference have been established in the animate matter kingdom with reproductive intelligence, the plant life kingdom, at different levels and different depths. To function at these levels and to use these points of reference, all you need is a sincere desire to solve problems. Your mind will automatically seek out these points of reference where you will perceive and become aware of information you can use to solve such problems. And this is so.

PROGRAM MENTAL VIDEO FOR RELATIONSHIPS

Programming a technique, the MentalVideo Technique that you can use for problem solving.

Whenever you need to solve a problem with the MentalVideo Technique, enter level 1 with the 3 to 1 method when you are in bed and ready to go to sleep. Once you are at your level, review the MentalVideo that you created of the problem previously when you were at beta.

After you have reviewed the problem, mentally convert the problem into a project. Then create, with imagination, a MentalVideo of the solution.

The MentalVideo of the solution should contain a step-by-step procedure of how you desire the project to be resolved.

After both of the MentalVideos have been completed, go to sleep with the intention of delivering the MentalVideos to your tutor while you sleep. Take for granted that the delivery will be made.

During the next three days, look for indications that point to the solution. Every time you think of the project, think of the solution that you created in the MentalVideo, in a past tense sense.

POST EFFECTS—PREVIEW OF NEXT SESSION

You have practiced entering deep, healthy levels of mind. In your next session, you will enter a deeper, healthier level of mind, faster and easier than this time.

POST EFFECTS—SPECIAL

Every time you function at these levels of the mind and at these points of reference, you will receive beneficial effects physically and mentally.

You may use these levels of the mind and these points of reference to help yourself physically and mentally.

You may use these levels of the mind and these points of reference to help your loved ones, physically and mentally.

You may use these levels of the mind and these points of reference to help any human being who needs help, physically and mentally.

You will never use these levels of the mind or these points of reference to harm any human being; if this be your intention, you will not be able to function within these levels of the mind, nor will you be able to use these points of reference.

You will always use these levels of the mind and these points of reference in a constructive, creative manner for all that is good, honest, pure, clean, and positive. And this is so.

You will continue to strive to take part in constructive and creative activities to make this a better world to live in, so that when we move on, we shall have left behind a better world for those who follow. You will consider the whole of humanity, depending on their ages, as fathers or mothers, brothers or sisters, sons or daughters. You are a superior human being; you have greater understanding, compassion, and patience with others.

BRING OUT

In a moment, I am going to count from 1 to 5 and cause a sound with my fingers. At that moment, you will open your eyes, be wide awake, feeling fine and in perfect health, feeling better than before. You will have no ill effects whatsoever in your head, no headache; no ill effects whatsoever in your hearing, no buzzing in your ears; no ill effects whatsoever in your vision and eyesight; vision, eyesight, and hearing improve every time you function at these levels of mind.

1—2—coming out slowly now.

3—at the count of 5, you will open your eyes, be wide awake, feeling fine and in perfect health, feeling better than before, feeling the way you feel when you have slept the right amount of revitalizing, refreshing, relaxing, healthy, wonderful sleep.

4—5 (snap fingers) eyes open, wide awake, feeling fine and in perfect health, feeling better than before.

THIS CONCLUDES THE PROJECTION TO TREE AND INTO LEAVES EXERCISE FOR JOSÉ SILVA'S ULTRAMIND ESP SYSTEMS.

CHAPTER 18

Mental Projection into Animal Life

Prerequisite: Projection into Plant Life Exercise

José Silva advised practicing the Centering Exercise prior to each of the five mental projection exercises.

Please read through the "Impression of New Material" first, before you go to your level, so you will know what to expect. This is known as "preconditioning."

For this exercise, use an animal you are familiar with, and that is healthy. It doesn't matter where the animal is located; no need to have it in the room with you.

Allow yourself enough time to complete the entire exercise, about 22 minutes. Turn off all communications devices and ask people not to disturb you so you can go through the entire exercise uninterrupted.

Here is the complete Anatomy of a Pet exercise:

MENTAL VIDEO PRACTICE SESSION

Let us, at beta with eyes open, mentally create, with visualization, a MentalVideo of a problem or a situation concerning business.

Include everything that belongs to the animate matter kingdom. Animate matter means everything that contains life. The MentalVideo must include everything animate that concerns the problem.

After having completed the MentalVideo of the problem, use visualization to review it at beta, with your eyes closed.

Mental Projection to Animal Life

DEEPENING (physical relaxation at level 3)
We will start this exercise with the 3 to 1 method.

Find a comfortable position, close your eyes, take a deep breath and while exhaling, mentally repeat and visualize the number 3 three times. (pause)

To help you learn to relax physically at level 3, I am going to direct your attention to different parts of your body.

(**Instructor**: Pause after every mention.)

Relax your scalp; relax your forehead; relax your eyes; relax your face; relax your throat; relax your shoulders; relax your chest externally and internally; relax your abdominal area externally and internally; relax your thighs; relax your knees; relax your calves; relax your feet.

You are now at a deeper, healthier level of mind, deeper than before. This is your physical relaxation level 3. Whenever you mentally repeat and visualize the number 3, your body will relax as completely as you are now, and more so every time you practice.

DEEPENING (mental relaxation at level 2)

To enter mental relaxation level 2, take a deep breath and while exhaling mentally repeat and visualize the number 2 three times, and you are at level 2, a deeper level than 3. (pause) Level 2 is for mental relaxation, where noises will not distract you. Instead, noises will help you to relax mentally more and more. To improve mental relaxation at level 2, practice visualizing tranquil and passive scenes. (pause)

TO ENTER YOUR CENTER

Take another deep breath and while exhaling, mentally repeat and visualize number 1 three times. (pause)

You are now at level 1, a deeper, healthier level of mind where you can function from your center.

DEEPENING (routine cycle)

To help you enter a deeper, healthier level of mind, I am going to count from 10 to 1. On each descending number, you will feel yourself going deeper and you will enter a deeper, healthier level of mind.

10—9—feel going deeper,

8—7—6—deeper and deeper,

5—4—3—deeper and deeper,

2—1

You are now at a deeper, healthier level of mind, deeper than before.

It is a wonderful feeling to be deeply relaxed, a very healthy state of being.

EFFECTIVE SENSORY PROJECTION STATEMENTS

Effective Sensory Projection statements for success.

I am now learning to attune my intelligence by developing my sensing faculties and to project them to any point or place on this planet so as to be aware of any actions taking place, if this is necessary and beneficial for humanity.

I am now learning to attune my intelligence by developing my sensing faculties and to project them to any point or place on any planet within the solar system, any solar system within the galaxy, and any galaxy within the universe so as to be aware of any actions taking place, if this is necessary and beneficial for humanity.

I am now learning to attune my intelligence by developing my sensing faculties and to project them to the different matter kingdoms: the inanimate matter kingdom, any of its levels and depths; the animate matter kingdom with reproductive intelligence, plant life and animal life, any of its levels and depths; and the animate matter kingdom with reproductive intelligence and an awareness of existence, the human body and mind kingdom, any of its levels and depths.

I am now learning to detect abnormalities whenever such abnormalities exist within any kingdom, any level, and any depth, if this is necessary and beneficial for humanity.

I am now learning to apply corrective measures and to bring back to normalcy any abnormality found within any kingdom, any level, and any depth, if this is necessary and beneficial for humanity.

Negative thoughts and negative suggestions have no influence over me at any level of the mind.

LAWS OF PROGRAMMING

The following laws are to be considered when programming:

You should do to others only what you like others to do to you.

The solution must help to make this planet a better place to live.

It must be the best for everybody concerned.

It must help at least two or more persons.

It must be within the possibility area.

PRINCIPLES TO KEEP IN MIND WHEN PROGRAMMING

The following principles apply to programming.

Objective physical communication takes place at the beta, left brain dimension using the objective—physical—senses. The hearing is used for perception, and the voice is used for transmission.

Subjective—mental—communication takes place at your center, the alpha, right brain dimension, by using the subjective senses. Visualization is used for perception, and imagination is used for transmission.

In the objective—physical—dimension, the past is behind us, the present is our present position, and the future is ahead of us.

In the subjective—mental—dimension, the past is to your right, the present is centered straight ahead, and the future is to your left.

IMPRESSION OF NEW MATERIAL (programming)

We will continue programming Effective Sensory Projection for your success, and continue programming information with the use of mental projection for your benefit. We will establish subjective points of reference in the animate matter kingdom with reproductive intelligence, the animal life kingdom, at different levels and depths; the "anatomy of a pet."

At the count of 3, mentally project yourself to the center of your living room, facing the south wall. 1—2—3 (snap fingers). You are now standing at the center of your living room, facing the south wall.

At the count of 3, mentally project your pet onto your Mental Screen. 1—2—3 (snap fingers). Now mentally move your pet in front of your Mental Screen, which is black and used as a background. (pause) Your pet is facing you; notice how the pet stands out against the black screen; (pause) mentally turn your pet to the left; (pause) turn the pet away from you; (pause) turn the pet to the right; (pause) place the pet facing you. (pause)

At the count of 3, the color of the screen will change to red. 1—2—3 (snap fingers). The screen is now red; study your pet; how does the pet stand out against a red background? (pause)

At the count of 3, the color of the screen will change to green. 1—2—3 (snap fingers). Study the pet against a green background. (pause)

At the count of 3, the color of the screen will change to blue. 1—2—3 (snap fingers). Now study the pet against a blue background. (pause) Whatever you perceive with your imagination at this dimension, you can use as a point of reference in the future.

The color of your Mental Screen will now change back to green (snap fingers), back to red (snap fingers), back to black (snap fingers).

Now mentally bring your pet closer, close enough to touch, noticing how the pet appears to become bigger as it gets closer.

(pause) Now objectively extend your arms and hold the pet by the head, one hand on each side. (pause) Study the head from several angles from this outer point of view. Whatever you perceive with your imagination at this dimension, you can use as a point of reference in the future.

Observe the eyes, (pause) the nose, (pause) the ears, (pause) the fur or outer covering. (pause) Focus your attention on the pet's forehead. (pause) At the count of 3, we will mentally enter the bone structure level of this kingdom. 1—2—3 (snap fingers). We are now at the bone structure level. Desire to perceive and imagine a bone or bones. (pause) Bring back a memory when you have seen a skull. (pause) Study the pet's skull from several angles. (pause) Whatever you perceive with your imagination at this dimension, you can use as a point of reference in the future.

Focus your attention on the pet's forehead. (pause) At the count of 3, we will enter the brain cell level. 1—2—3 (snap fingers). Desire to perceive and imagine brain cells or brain matter. (pause) Bring back a memory when you have seen a brain in a picture or on a chart. (pause) Study the brain from several angles. (pause) Whatever you perceive with your imagination at this dimension, you can use as a point of reference in the future.

At the count of 3, we will go back to the bone structure level. 1—2—3 (snap fingers). Now at the count of 3, we will again be at the outer level of this kingdom. 1—2—3 (snap fingers). We are now at the outer level of this kingdom. Again observe the eyes, the nose, the ears, the fur or outer covering.

Now mentally move the pet a little higher and hold it by the rib cage; objectively place one hand on each side of the rib cage. (pause) Now focus your attention on the center of the pet's chest. (pause) At the count of 3, we will enter the bone structure level.

1—2—3 (snap fingers). Desire to perceive and imagine the ribs of your pet; (pause) now the spinal column; (pause) study the complete skeletal body. (pause) You can raise or lower the skeleton to any position or angle and it will remain in that position or angle. (pause) Whatever you perceive with your imagination at this dimension, you can use as a point of reference in the future.

Now focus your attention on the chest. (pause) At the count of 3, we will enter the heart tissue level. 1—2—3 (snap fingers). Desire to perceive and imagine a heart. (pause) Bring back a memory when you have seen a heart. (pause) Study the heart from several angles. (pause) Whatever you perceive with your imagination at this dimension, you can use as a point of reference in the future.

Again focus your attention on the heart. (pause) At the count of 3, we will sense the heart transparent. 1—2—3 (snap fingers). Bring back a memory of having seen a picture of a transparent heart; imagine what it would look like. (pause) Whatever you perceive with your imagination at this dimension, you can use as a point of reference in the future.

At the count of 3, we will enter the lung tissue level. 1—2—3 (snap fingers). Desire to perceive and imagine two lungs. (pause) Bring back a memory when you have seen pictures of lungs. (pause) Study the lungs of this pet from several angles. (pause) Whatever you perceive with your imagination at this dimension, you can use as a point of reference in the future.

At the count of 3, we will enter the kidney tissue level. 1—2—3 (snap fingers). Desire to perceive and imagine two kidneys. (pause) Bring back a memory of having seen kidneys, such as in anatomy book pictures, or at the meat market. (pause) Study your pet's kidneys from several angles. (pause) Whatever you perceive with your imagination at this dimension, you can use as a point of reference in the future.

At the count of 3, we will enter the liver tissue level. 1—2—3 (snap fingers). Desire to perceive and imagine a liver. (pause) Study your pet's liver from several angles. (pause) Whatever you perceive with your imagination at this dimension, you can use as a point of reference in the future.

At the count of 3, we will go back to the kidney level. 1—2—3 (snap fingers). Now back to the lung level (snap fingers), now back to the heart level (snap fingers), now back to the skeletal level (snap fingers), now to the outer level of this dimension (snap fingers). Now mentally place your pet in front of your Mental Screen; (pause) now mentally turn your pet to your left; (pause) now turn it away from you; (pause) now to your right; (pause) now toward you. (pause) Change the color of the screen to red (snap fingers). Change the color of the screen to green (snap fingers). Now change the color to blue (snap fingers).

We will change the color of the screen back to green (snap fingers), back to red (snap fingers), back to black (snap fingers). Now imagine your pet in perfect health. (pause) Now cause your pet to disappear from the scene (snap fingers). Your pet has now disappeared from the scene.

Whatever you perceive with your imagination at this dimension, you can use as points of reference in the future. It is now an accomplished fact that subjective points of reference have been established at different levels and depths of the animate matter kingdom with reproductive intelligence, the animal life kingdom. To function at these levels and to use these points of reference, all you need is a sincere desire to solve problems. Your mind will automatically seek out these points of reference, where you will perceive and become aware of information that you can use to solve such problems. And this is so.

PROGRAM MENTALVIDEO FOR BUSINESS

Programming a technique, the MentalVideo Technique that you can use for problem solving.

Whenever you need to solve a problem with the MentalVideo Technique, enter level 1 with the 3 to 1 method when you are in bed and ready to go to sleep. Once you are at your level, review the MentalVideo that you created of the problem previously when you were at beta.

After you have reviewed the problem, mentally convert the problem into a project. Then create, with imagination, a MentalVideo of the solution.

The MentalVideo of the solution should contain a step-by-step procedure of how you desire the project to be resolved.

After both of the MentalVideos have been completed, go to sleep with the intention of delivering the MentalVideos to your tutor while you sleep. Take for granted that the delivery will be made.

During the next three days, look for indications that point to the solution. Every time you think of the project, think of the solution that you created in the MentalVideo, in a past tense sense.

POST EFFECTS—PREVIEW OF NEXT SESSION

You have practiced entering deep, healthy levels of mind. In your next session, you will enter a deeper, healthier level of mind, faster and easier than this time.

POST EFFECTS—SPECIAL

Every time you function at these levels of the mind and at these points of reference, you will receive beneficial effects physically and mentally.

You may use these levels of the mind and these points of reference to help yourself physically and mentally.

You may use these levels of the mind and these points of reference to help your loved ones, physically and mentally.

You may use these levels of the mind and these points of reference to help any human being who needs help, physically and mentally.

You will never use these levels of the mind or these points of reference to harm any human being; if this be your intention, you will not be able to function within these levels of the mind, nor will you be able to use these points of reference.

You will always use these levels of the mind and these points of reference in a constructive, creative manner for all that is good, honest, pure, clean, and positive. And this is so.

You will continue to strive to take part in constructive and creative activities to make this a better world to live in, so that when we move on, we shall have left behind a better world for those who follow. You will consider the whole of humanity, depending on their ages, as fathers or mothers, brothers or sisters, sons or daughters. You are a superior human being; you have greater understanding, compassion, and patience with others.

BRING OUT

In a moment, I am going to count from 1 to 5 and cause a sound with my fingers. At that moment, you will open your eyes, be wide awake, feeling fine and in perfect health, feeling better than before. You will have no ill effects whatsoever in your head, no headache; no ill effects whatsoever in your hearing, no buzzing in your ears; no ill effects whatsoever in your vision and eyesight; vision, eyesight, and hearing improve every time you function at these levels of mind.

1—2—coming out slowly now.

3—at the count of 5, you will open your eyes, be wide awake, feeling fine and in perfect health, feeling better than before, feeling the way you feel when you have slept the right amount of revitalizing, refreshing, relaxing, healthy, wonderful sleep.

4—5 (snap fingers) eyes open, wide awake, feeling fine and in perfect health, feeling better than before.

THIS CONCLUDES THE ANATOMY OF A PET EXERCISE FOR JOSÉ SILVA'S ULTRAMIND ESP SYSTEMS.

CHAPTER 19

How to Practice Psychometry

Prerequisite: Projection into Animal Life Exercise

The vibrations from your aura—the various energies that radiate from your brain and body—penetrate objects within your presence, and affect the internal vibrations of objects within your aura range.

Your body radiation charges up the objects with your own frequencies. When you touch a ring your vibrations penetrate the ring and it becomes an extension of you. Any time later, when someone touches the ring, and desires to obtain information, that person can obtain information from those vibrations in the ring.

Your mind uses the vibrations in an object to help you tune in to the person. Whenever you desire to obtain information on that person, it will be helpful if you have an object from that person. When you sense the vibrations within that object, that will help your mind to be able to tune in to that person to obtain the information that you need.

Preparing to Practice Psychometry

Find a friend or somebody that you know, and tell them that you need objects from two different people, the people who carried the objects with them, have had the objects with them in their physical presence for a while.

It could be a driver's license, maybe some keys that they don't use anymore but they carried for a long time, or a lucky coin, or something like that. Something that they have had with them.

Ask them to put the object in an envelope, so you can't see it, and don't tell you who it came from. Don't tell you who the person is. It's great if it's somebody you don't know. It's also fine if it's somebody you know, as long as they don't tell you who it is, and you don't know who it came from, and you can't just logically guess who they would have gotten the objects from.

Then ask the person to describe themselves on a piece of paper, with information like this:
- whether they are male or female,
- their height and weight,
- the color of hair,
- the color of eyes,
- their complexion,
- what their personality is like,
- hobbies,
- do they have children, pets.

They need to write down at least enough information so when you're projecting into the object mentally, and you start detecting all this information, you have enough to compare with what they wrote down.

Then have them put the paper and the object into the envelope and seal it, and then your friend can bring it to you.

Your Psychometry Practice Session

When you are ready to practice, hold the envelope containing the object in the palm of your left hand and decide what information you would like to detect. Then, enter your level with the 3 to 1 Method and desire to detect that information.

Usually the information that you perceive immediately is the correct information.

When you finish, open the envelope and compare your answers with the information that was provided to you.

This will help you to gain confidence, and establish points of reference so you can be confident that you are doing the right thing.

On average, an untrained person, when guessing, will be correct one out of five times.

On average, a good psychic will be correct four out of five times.

Once you have determined that you are correct more than one out of five times, then you are on your way to developing superior intuition.

Psychometry can help you locate missing persons.

You can also charge up objects with your energy and leave with people to serve as reminders of you.

A word of caution: Be sure you are telling the truth because if you are trying to take advantage of somebody, that's the message that will be impressed on the item you leave with them.

We cover these techniques in the Advanced ESP Techniques chapter in Part 5 of this Master Course.

CHAPTER 20

Mental Projection into Human Life

Prerequisite: Projection into Animal Life Exercise

José Silva advised practicing the Centering Exercise prior to each of the five mental projection exercises.

Please read through the "Impression of New Material" first, before you go to your level, so you will know what to expect. This is known as "preconditioning."

Please choose a subject who is in good health so you can establish points of reference for a healthy human body. This can be a relative or a friend, someone whose face you can recall with the least effort.

You might find it beneficial to look at an anatomy chart if you are not sure of what the various parts of the body look like. You can find a lot of anatomy charts on the internet.

Here are some of the procedures and techniques mentioned in this mental exercise:

Use your hands. My best friend in college was blind, and through him I met most of the other blind students. On first meeting, many of them asked if they could feel my face so they would know what I looked like. They touched my face very lightly and only for a few seconds. That was enough.

So if you are having trouble recalling exactly what your subject looks like, raise your hands physically and imagine feeling their face, hair, nose, ears, lips.

Finger-Snapping Controls were first used in the Projection into Metals exercise in Chapter 16. To increase the illumination or amount or size of anything, just snap the fingers of your right hand slightly, and expect the change to take place. For a decrease, or to return anything back to its original state, snap the fingers of your left hand slightly, and expect the change to take place.

Imagine superimposing the subject's head over your own, as though you are putting on a helmet, in order to test their senses. Wait until you have some experience working on physical health problems before you work on mental health problems.

Soul mold refers to the subjective blueprint for the body. When you imagine a diseased organ returning to perfect health and you visualize the organ functioning perfectly, you are reinforcing the soul mold.

While the doctor works from the outside in using physical means, you can work from the inside out. Matter is attracted to conform to the soul mold.

Clear your mind for a moment of time when conducting tests. That means to think of something different, such as an errand you need to run or something you need to do later. Then go back to your investigation and start thinking again to figure out the answer. The first impression that comes is usually the strongest and the correct one.

The Time Mechanism Device: Imagine that the palm of your left hand is like the face of a clock, and as you hold it up, you use the forefinger of your right hand to turn the hands of the clock backward or forward. Imagine that each revolution represents one unit of time: a minute, an hour, a day, a week, a month, a year, a decade, a century . . . whatever you desire.

At the conclusion of the exercise we will instruct you to count yourself out of level on your own.

Projection to Human Anatomy Exercise

Allow yourself enough time to complete the entire exercise, about 40 minutes. Turn off all communications devices and ask people not to disturb you so you can go through the entire exercise uninterrupted. If you stop before the end, you will need to start over again at the beginning.

MENTAL VIDEO PRACTICE SESSION

Let us, at beta with eyes open, mentally create, with visualization, a MentalVideo of a problem or a situation concerning creativity, spirituality, and personal growth.

Include everything that belongs to the animate matter kingdom. Animate matter means everything that contains life. The MentalVideo must include everything animate that concerns the problem.

After having completed the MentalVideo of the problem, use visualization to review it at beta, with your eyes closed.

DEEPENING (physical relaxation at level 3)

We will start this exercise with the 3 to 1 method.

Find a comfortable position, close your eyes, take a deep

breath and while exhaling, mentally repeat and visualize the number 3 three times. (pause)

To help you learn to relax physically at level 3, I am going to direct your attention to different parts of your body.

(**Instructor**: Pause after every mention.)

Relax your scalp; relax your forehead; relax your eyes; relax your face; relax your throat; relax your shoulders; relax your chest externally and internally; relax your abdominal area externally and internally; relax your thighs; relax your knees; relax your calves; relax your feet.

You are now at a deeper, healthier level of mind, deeper than before. This is your physical relaxation level 3. Whenever you mentally repeat and visualize the number 3, your body will relax as completely as you are now, and more so every time you practice.

DEEPENING (mental relaxation at level 2)

To enter mental relaxation level 2, take a deep breath and while exhaling mentally repeat and visualize the number 2 three times, and you are at level 2, a deeper level than 3. (pause) Level 2 is for mental relaxation, where noises will not distract you. Instead, noises will help you to relax mentally more and more.

To improve mental relaxation at level 2, practice visualizing tranquil and passive scenes. (pause)

TO ENTER YOUR CENTER

Take another deep breath and while exhaling, mentally repeat and visualize number 1 three times. (pause)

You are now at level 1, a deeper, healthier level of mind where you can function from your center.

DEEPENING (routine cycle)

To help you enter a deeper, healthier level of mind, I am going to count from 10 to 1. On each descending number, you will feel yourself going deeper and you will enter a deeper, healthier level of mind.

10—9—feel going deeper,

8—7—6—deeper and deeper,

5—4—3—deeper and deeper,

2—1

You are now at a deeper, healthier level of mind, deeper than before.

It is a wonderful feeling to be deeply relaxed, a very healthy state of being.

EFFECTIVE SENSORY PROJECTION STATEMENTS

Effective Sensory Projection statements for success.

I am now learning to attune my intelligence by developing my sensing faculties and to project them to any point or place on this planet so as to be aware of any actions taking place, if this is necessary and beneficial for humanity.

I am now learning to attune my intelligence by developing my sensing faculties and to project them to any point or place on any planet within the solar system, any solar system within the galaxy, and any galaxy within the universe so as to be aware of any actions taking place, if this is necessary and beneficial for humanity.

I am now learning to attune my intelligence by developing my sensing faculties and to project them to the different matter kingdoms: the inanimate matter kingdom, any of its levels and depths; the animate matter kingdom with reproductive intelligence, plant life and animal life, any of its levels and depths; and the animate matter kingdom with reproductive intelligence and an awareness of existence, the human body and mind kingdom, any of its levels and depths.

I am now learning to detect abnormalities whenever such abnormalities exist within any kingdom, any level, and any depth, if this is necessary and beneficial for humanity.

I am now learning to apply corrective measures and to bring back to normalcy any abnormality found within any kingdom, any level, and any depth, if this is necessary and beneficial for humanity.

Negative thoughts and negative suggestions have no influence over me at any level of the mind.

LAWS OF PROGRAMMING

The following laws are to be considered when programming:

You should do to others only what you like others to do to you.

The solution must help to make this planet a better place to live.

It must be the best for everybody concerned.

It must help at least two or more persons.

It must be within the possibility area.

PRINCIPLES TO KEEP IN MIND WHEN PROGRAMMING

The following principles apply to programming.

Objective physical communication takes place at the beta, left brain dimension using the objective—physical—senses. The hearing is used for perception, and the voice is used for transmission.

Subjective—mental—communication takes place at your center, the alpha, right brain dimension by using the subjective senses. Visualization is used for perception, and imagination is used for transmission.

In the objective—physical—dimension, the past is behind us, the present is our present position, and the future is ahead of us.

In the subjective—mental—dimension, the past is to your right, the present is centered straight ahead, and the future is to your left.

IMPRESSION OF NEW MATERIAL (programming)

We will now program Effective Sensory Projection for your success. We will establish subjective points of reference at the animate matter kingdom with reproductive intelligence and an awareness of existence; that is, we will program points of reference in the human body and mind kingdom, at its different levels and different depths, as we study the human anatomy from a psychic point of view.

At this time, select a relative, a friend, or a person whose face you can remember with the least effort. We will refer to this person as "the subject." Now recall the subject's face. (pause) At the count of 3, you will project the subject onto your

Mental Screen. 1—2—3 (snap fingers). The subject is now on your Mental Screen. Now mentally move the subject away from the Mental Screen so that the screen can be used as a background. The color of the screen is black. (pause) Now mentally turn the subject's body so its left side is toward you; (pause) now turn the subject's back toward you; (pause) now turn the subject's right side toward you; (pause) now turn the subject to be facing you. (pause)

Notice how the body of the subject stands out against a black screen. (pause) The screen will now change to red (snap fingers); the screen is now red; notice how your subject stands out against the red screen. (pause) The screen will now change to green (snap fingers); the screen is now green. Notice how your subject stands out against a green screen. (pause) The screen will now change to blue (snap fingers); the screen is now blue; notice how your subject stands out against a blue screen. (pause) The color of the screen will now change back to green (snap fingers), now back to red (snap fingers), now back to black (snap fingers).

At the count of 3, you will mentally bring your subject close enough to touch. 1—2—3 (snap fingers). The subject is now close enough to touch. At the count of 3 you will objectively extend your arms and place your hands, one on each side of the head. 1—2—3 (snap fingers). Objectively place your hands one on each side of the subject's head, your right hand over the left ear, and your left hand over the subject's right ear. Now study your subject's face, the facial features: the hair, eyes, eyebrows, nose, cheeks, the character of the face. (pause) Whatever you perceive with your imagination at this dimension, you can use as a point of reference in the future.

Now concentrate on your subject's forehead, and at the count of 3, we will enter the bone structure level within the human kingdom. 1–2–3 (snap fingers). Desire to detect, through visualization or imagination, bone; bring back a memory of bone, its shape, color, and appearance. (pause) Now concentrate on the skull of your subject; study it from several angles, from the left, from the back, and from the right. (pause) Whatever you perceive with your imagination at this dimension, you can use as a point of reference in the future.

Now again concentrate your attention on your subject's forehead area, and at the count of 3, we will enter the brain structure level. 1–2–3 (snap fingers). Desire to detect, through visualization or imagination, a brain; recall your previous experience of how a brain looks; perhaps you have seen pictures of a brain. (pause) Study the brain from different angles, desiring to detect the various colors of the brain such as gray in the front part, pink in the mid-part, and dark red in the back part. (pause) Whatever you perceive with your imagination at this dimension, you can use as a point of reference in the future.

When there is brain damage, you will get an impression of black areas or spots. To help in the solution of this problem, erase the dark area or spot and form and project an impression of a healthy brain, and it is so. When you imagine a damaged area, get further impressions of the connecting nerves, which you can then follow to the possible corresponding malfunctions of the body. Damaged nerves should impress you as being oval and flat and dark in color. Healthy nerves will appear transparent and roundish. Some nerves, like those in the sen-so-ri-motor system, cross over from one side of the brain to the opposite side of the body. (pause)

Concentrate your attention on the front part of the brain again. At the count of 3, we will return to the bone structure level. 1—2—3 (snap fingers). Get an impression of a skull. At the count of 3 we will return to the outer level. 1—2—3 (snap fingers). We are at the outer level. Get an impression of the hair, the face, the eyes, and eyebrows. To test the senses, you can imagine that you are superimposing the subject's head over your own, as though you were putting on a helmet. Then you will test your own senses, and whatever you feel reflects the condition of your subject. While your subject's head is superimposed over your own, you can ask what kind of problem your subject has. You may ask whether it is psychological, or physiological, and then clear your mind for a moment of time. Whatever impression comes to you immediately after this will tell you the problem of your subject. You will then concentrate in this particular area. Whatever you perceive with your imagination at this dimension, you can use as a point of reference in the future. Remember, whenever you put the subject's head over your own, to remove it when you have completed your investigation.

Now raise the body, still facing you, and place your hands on each side of the rib cage. (pause) Begin concentrating on the center of the chest. At the count of 3 we will again enter the bone structure level within the human kingdom. 1—2—3 (snap fingers). You are now at the bone structure level. Desire to detect, through visualization or imagination, the skeletal structure of your subject: the rib cage, the spinal column, the arms and legs, and the hip bones. (pause) We are now able to detect abnormalities at this level and, in the case of arthritis, for example, you will detect a powdery substance collecting on the joints of the fingers, and sometimes the wrists, elbows, shoulder joints, and even the spinal column. The same substance will be evident in other joints where arthritis may occur, such as the toes, ankles, knees, and hipbones. (pause) You will also be able to detect fractures, old and new. To determine when a fracture took place, use your Time Mechanism Device, and go back in time until the perceived fracture disappears, and you know then when the fracture occurred. Whatever you perceive with your imagination at this dimension, you can use as a point of reference in the future.

Now again concentrate on the center of the chest. At the count of 3, we will enter the heart tissue level within the human kingdom. 1—2—3 (snap fingers). We are now at the heart tissue level. Desire to detect, through visualization or imagination, your subject's heart. (pause) Recall previous impressions and pictures of a heart, and recall how it operates. (pause) Imagine this heart, which belongs to your subject; imagine it from an external point of view; sense it; know it is there; feel it. (pause) Whatever you perceive with your imagination at this dimension, you can use as a point of reference in the future.

At the count of 3, the heart will become transparent. 1—2—3 (snap fingers). It is now transparent; imagine how the valves function. (pause) Sometimes you will get the impression of an enlarged heart, or erratic beating, or scar tissue formations, and in some cases malfunctioning valves. (pause) Whatever you perceive with your imagination at this dimension, you can use as a point of reference in the future.

To test for blood pressure, fold the fingers of your hand around an artery near the heart. Use your imagination to feel the intensity of the pulsations. (pause) If you get the impression of strong pulsations, there is high blood pressure; the strength of pulsations can also indicate normal, or weak, pulsations or pressure. If you get the impression that the artery gives and contracts, that it is flexible, then there is no hardening of the arteries. An impression of no flexibility means hardening of the arteries. (pause)

To test for blood chemistry, mentally draw a sample of the subject's blood and put it in an imaginary test tube. Then agitate the blood sample, and before stopping decide the purpose of the test; once you have decided to test for the percentage of white blood cells, or sugar content, or cholesterol, or foreign chemicals, stop agitating the sample; let it settle. You will detect two different colors of blood chemistry; the less dominant color will indicate the substance you are testing for. Once you have detected what you are testing for, you will mentally ask yourself whether you are impressed with high, low, or normal content. Then clear your mind for a moment, and the first impression you receive is usually the strongest and the right one. You can repeat this operation with the same blood sample for the rest of the test. Whatever you perceive with your imagination at this dimension, you can use as a point of reference in the future.

At the count of 3, we will enter the lung tissue level within the human kingdom. 1—2—3 (snap fingers). Desire to detect, through visualization or imagination, two lungs as they expand and contract; one lung could be a little larger than the other; this is sometimes normal. (pause) You may become aware of occasional lung problems such as fluid at the bottom of the lungs, or of more serious conditions such as infections, tumors, perforations, loss of elasticity, asthma, and other detectable states. Whatever you perceive with your imagination at this dimension, you can use as a point of reference in the future.

Sometimes portions of a lung or the complete lung have to be removed through surgery. When this happens, you will detect a lighter color on the portion of lung that has been removed, or the complete lung when removed may be lighter. Any portion of the body that has been amputated will impress you as being lighter in color than the rest of the body. Once you have found a malfunctioning part of the body, sense it changing back to proper functioning, and let this be your final impression.

At the count of 3, we will enter the stomach tissue level within the human kingdom. 1–2–3 (snap fingers). Desire to detect, through visualization or imagination, your subject's stomach; recall your previous experience for an accurate impression of a stomach. (pause) Whatever you perceive with your imagination at this dimension, you can use as a point of reference in the future.

Some of the more common problems of the stomach area are ulcers, tumors, obstructions, and the improper balance of gastric juices. In the case of surgery, when a portion of the stomach has been removed, you will get the impression of an entire stomach with the missing part sensed in a lighter shade or color that contrasts with the rest of the stomach.

At the count of 3, we will enter the level to sense the intestinal tract. 1–2–3 (snap fingers). Desire to detect, through visualization or imagination, the intestinal tract as it begins at the outlet of the stomach; the first part of the small intestine is called the du–o–de–num. (pause) Some of the problems of the intestines are much the same as those of the stomach, and many of these same problems carry over to the large intestine at the lower right side of the trunk of the body, where the appendix is located. (pause) Whatever you perceive with your

imagination at this dimension, you can use as a point of reference in the future.

At the count of 3, we will concentrate on the pancreas, at
that particular tissue level. 1—2—3 (snap fingers). Desire to
detect, through visualization or imagination, the pancreas: it is
slightly below and behind the stomach. It is an elongated gland
that feeds its digestive juices through a duct into the du-o-de-
num. (pause) An obstructed duct could prevent the enzymes
from entering the du-o-de-num. The pancreas contains islands
of cells that produce a hormone called insulin that is released
directly into the blood stream. An impression of black spots, or
islands, on the pancreas could indicate diabetes. Light spots, or
islands, on the pancreas could indicate hypoglycemia. (pause)
Whatever you perceive with your imagination at this dimension, you can use as a point of reference in the future.

A final impression of a properly functioning and healthy
pancreas is recommended for better health.

At the count of 3, we will enter the liver tissue level within
the human kingdom. 1—2—3 (snap fingers). Desire to detect,
through visualization or imagination, the liver, The liver is a
little higher than the pancreas, and to the right in the person's
body. (pause) It has been said by psychics that if the liver gives
a shiny impression, it is healthy. If dull, a problem exists. There
could be one of several things wrong. There could be an enlarge-
ment of the liver, tumors, or infections. (pause) Whatever you
perceive with your imagination at this dimension, you can use
as a point of reference in the future.

At the count of 3, we will enter the gall bladder level within
the human kingdom. 1—2—3 (snap fingers). Desire to detect,
through visualization or imagination, the gall bladder. (pause)

The gall bladder is attached to the liver. It has a duct that joins the pancreatic duct to form the common duct into the du-o-de-num. (pause) Stone formations could exist in the duct of any gland. When you perceive an impression of stone formations in the gall bladder or in any duct, imagine going through the process of crushing the stones into a fine powder with your fingers, and imagine the powder dissolving in the gland's secretions. Your last impression of the gall bladder should be a healthy one with no stone formations. (pause) Whatever you perceive with your imagination at this dimension, you can use as a point of reference in the future.

At the count of 3, we will enter the kidney tissue level within the human kingdom. 1—2—3 (snap fingers). Desire to detect, through visualization or imagination, two kidneys; you have seen pictures of kidneys before; get an impression of them as being solid, from an outer point of view. (pause) Sometimes one kidney is a little larger than the other, and sometimes one is a little higher, but this could be a normal condition. (pause) Whatever you perceive with your imagination at this dimension, you can use as a point of reference in the future.

At the count of 3, we will perceive the kidneys being transparent. 1—2—3 (snap fingers). Desire to sense the kidneys transparent. If you detect these filtering systems as processing unequally or differently from each other, then something could be wrong, such as an infection. An infection could travel up from the bladder to the kidney, or from the kidney to the bladder. Stone formations also could hinder the functioning of a kidney. When this is the case, imagine crushing the stone formations into fine powder with your fingers and imagine the powder dissolving in the urine. (pause) Whatever you perceive with your imagination at this dimension, you can use as a point of reference in the future.

When you get an impression that both kidneys are not functioning quite well, but you are not sure why, then compare the subject's kidneys to those of a healthy person who has no kidney problems. The final impression should always be one of health.

At the count of 3, we will go back to the gall bladder level. 1—2—3 (snap fingers), to the liver level (snap fingers), to the pancreas level (snap fingers), to the intestinal tract level (snap fingers), to the stomach level (snap fingers), to the lung level (snap fingers), to the heart level (snap fingers), to the skeletal body level (snap fingers), now back to the outer level (snap fingers).

We are now at the outer level of the human kingdom. Here you can study the outer skin, by desiring to perceive it through visualization or imagination. (pause) You can detect skin problems, such as infections, allergies, tumors, injuries, or scars. (pause) Whatever you perceive with your imagination at this dimension, you can use as a point of reference in the future.

Now project your subject back in front of the screen. (pause) Mentally turn the subject's body so the subject's left side faces you. (pause) Now turn the subject's back toward you. (pause) Now the right side. (pause) Now allow the subject to face you. (pause)

Change the color of the screen to red (snap fingers). Change the color of the screen to green (snap fingers). Now change the color to blue (snap fingers).

The color of the screen will now change back to green (snap fingers), back to red (snap fingers), back to black (snap fingers). Now imagine your subject in perfect health. (pause) Now cause your subject to disappear from the screen (snap fingers). Your subject has now disappeared from the screen area.

Whatever you perceive with your imagination at this dimension, you can use as points of reference in the future. It is now an accomplished fact that you have established subjective points of reference in the animate matter kingdom having reproductive intelligence and an awareness of existence, and you understand how these points of reference apply to the human body and mind kingdom at its different levels and different depths. To function at these levels and to use these points of reference, all you need is a sincere desire to solve problems. Your mind will automatically seek out these points of reference, where you will perceive and become aware of information you can use to solve problems. And this is so.

PROGRAM THE MENTALVIDEO FOR CREATIVITY AND SPIRITUALITY

Programming a technique, the MentalVideo Technique that you can use for problem solving.

Whenever you need to solve a problem with the MentalVideo Technique, enter level 1 with the 3 to 1 method when you are in bed and ready to go to sleep. Once you are at your level, review the MentalVideo that you created of the problem previously when you were at beta.

After you have reviewed the problem, mentally convert the problem into a project. Then create, with imagination, a MentalVideo of the solution.

The MentalVideo of the solution should contain a step-by-step procedure of how you desire the project to be resolved.

After both of the MentalVideos have been completed, go to sleep with the intention of delivering the MentalVideos to your tutor while you sleep. Take for granted that the delivery will be made.

During the next three days, look for indications that point to the solution. Every time you think of the project, think of the solution that you created in the MentalVideo, in a past tense sense.

POST EFFECTS—PREVIEW OF NEXT SESSION

From this time forward, begin practicing problem cases with one or two others who have finished the series. Each should bring some cases to the practice session, and one will function as a psychic, another as the orientologist who will present the case, and the third as an observer who takes notes. The three can talk to one another at any time.

When you have worked at least 10 cases and you are satisfied with the results, then use only the 10 to 1 method for entering your clairvoyant level. When you have worked another 10 cases and you continue to be satisfied with the results, then use only the 3 to 1 method for entering your clairvoyant level.

When you have worked still another 10 cases and you continue to be satisfied with the results, then all you need to do is to close your eyes and take one deep breath and while exhaling, you will enter your clairvoyant level.

Once you are completely satisfied with your results, you can function with your eyes open when needed. Your desire to function at your clairvoyant level with your eyes open, will cause the so-called "daydream" mechanism to function at your clairvoyant level.

From then on your daydreaming will take place at your clair-voyant level, and to enter it just "daydream." At that time, con-trolled "daydreaming" will be "creative" and the "true reality."

POST EFFECTS—SPECIAL

Every time you function at these levels of the mind and at these points of reference, you will receive beneficial effects physically and mentally.

You may use these levels of the mind and these points of ref-erence to help yourself physically and mentally.

You may use these levels of the mind and these points of ref-erence to help your loved ones, physically and mentally.

You may use these levels of the mind and these points of ref-erence to help any human being who needs help, physically and mentally.

You will never use these levels of the mind or these points of reference to harm any human being; if this be your intention, you will not be able to function within these levels of the mind, nor will you be able to use these points of reference.

You will always use these levels of the mind and these points of reference in a constructive, creative manner for all that is good, honest, pure, clean, and positive. And this is so.

You will continue to strive to take part in constructive and creative activities to make this a better world to live in, so that when we move on, we shall have left behind a better world for those who follow. You will consider the whole of humanity, depending on their ages, as fathers or mothers, brothers or sis-ters, sons or daughters. You are a superior human being; you have greater understanding, compassion, and patience with others.

BRING OUT

I will now count from 1 to 3. At the count of 3, you will complete the coming out ritual; you will count from 1 to 10 and 1 to 3 to come out of your clairvoyant level feeling fine and in perfect health. 1—2—3 (snap fingers). Complete your coming out ritual on your own; take your time.

THIS CONCLUDES THE HUMAN ANATOMY EXERCISE FOR JOSÉ SILVA'S ULTRAMIND ESP SYSTEMS.

CHAPTER 21

Working Health Detection and Correction Cases

Prerequisite: Projection into Human Life Exercise

There are several ways to get health cases to work.

The best way is to partner with another Silva ESP student, perhaps a family member, or a friend. When you help one another, you both benefit. One way you both benefit is by getting cases to present to each other. Of course, you can also work cases on your own. We'll cover that in a moment.

Another source of cases is the news. When you see or hear a news story about someone sick or injured or killed, make a note of their name, age, location, and gender, so you can present it to your programming partner. If the news media doesn't report what injuries the person has, you can work a case on them yourself and maybe a later news report will have details you can use to confirm what you detected.

If you don't have someone you can work with, then you can get cases by simply asking people. You can ask family members, friends, even casual acquaintances.

When I first took the course, I was working in a small quick-printing shop. Many of our customers would have a cup of coffee and chat with us while we printed their material. Sometimes I would tell them that I worked with a group who liked to pray for people who were sick or injured, and asked if they knew someone we could pray for. Many of them did.

I told them we liked to pray for people twice: first without knowing what the problem is, then again after we know, and I had them write down the person's name, age, gender, and location on one side of a piece of paper, and their health problem on the other side. Then they would fold the paper, so I couldn't see the health problem, and give it to me.

I assured them that nobody would see this information except members of our group. Nobody ever turned down this offer, and some even asked if they could donate to our church. I declined, of course, and told them we feel it is more effective that way. In the United States it is also illegal to accept any remuneration for "healing" unless you have a license to do so, or belong to a church that practices holistic faith healing.

Standard Caseworking Procedure

If you have a partner who can present cases to you, here is the standard procedure for working health detection and correction cases.

José Silva recommends working in groups of two or three. One person is the psychic, another serves as the orientologist who presents the case to the psychic, and the third is an observer who takes notes.

Go to your center with the 3 to 1 method.

Review your most recent case when you were 100 percent successful. Recall how you felt. This will help you to reach the same state of mind again, and to be just as successful as you were then.

When you are ready, let the orientologist know.

Your orientologist will do a 10 to 1 countdown to ensure that you are at your clairvoyant level.

The orientologist presents the case to you.

Then you give a complete report of everything that you experience. Say everything that comes to mind. During this time, the orientologist does not give any feedback, but simply encourages you to continue talking and reporting everything.

After you have given a complete report, and while you are still at your clairvoyant level, the orientologist tells you about the case, confirming the "hits" that you had. If you mentioned something that the orientologist does not have any information about, then during the review, the orientologist will simply say, "I do not have that information; it could be so." If you detected some problems but missed some others, the orientologist can also tell you about the ones you did not detect.

With the help of the orientologist, establish points of reference for your hits. Notice how you perceived the information, and how you felt. What did you detect on your "hits"—a different color, shape, size? Remember to use your hands; this will help you detect problems. This kind of analysis will help you to recognize it when you encounter the same situation again.

Correct all of the problems that you detected (including those that the orientologist did not confirm), and also any others the orientologist might have told you about.

Clear your screen, relax, and work your next case in the same manner: detecting information, getting feedback, establishing points of reference, correcting the problems.

Usually students are comfortable working three or four cases before coming out of level. When you are finished with your session (after having worked one or more cases), your orientologist will read the following to you:

"Every time you enter this dimension with the sincere desire to help humanity, as you did this time, you will be helping yourself; your talents will increase and you will become more accurate every time. And this is so."

Come out of level 1 to 10 and 1 to 3.

This whole process typically takes about 15 minutes.

Discuss the case briefly.

How to Expand Your Experiences

When you are learning to work health cases, you should say whatever comes to mind. This is a practice session. You may feel as though you are making it up. This is the correct feeling, so say anything that occurs to you.

I was watching a caseworking session when one of the things the new student reported was that the subject had "cold feet." After the psychic had completed their report, the orientologist said she did not have any information about cold feet.

The psychic did not detect anything else out of the ordinary, so the orientologist provided feedback: The subject had a bad heart.

"Couldn't that cause cold feet sometimes?" I asked. "If the heart isn't pumping enough blood, maybe the extremities would get cold?"

The psychic said that very thing happened to her grandmother: She had a heart condition and she often complained of cold feet or hands.

"Perhaps that is your point of reference for a heart problem," I said, "because of your previous experience. Now let's see if we can get you another, more direct, point of reference."

Then I asked the orientologist if she had any additional information about the subject's heart—not to tell me what the information was, just whether she had any. She did, but she didn't tell us what she knew.

Then I instructed the psychic to go back to her level and check the heart to see if she could detect anything abnormal.

"Allow the possibility of afflictions and malfunctions to enter your mind," I told her. "In other words, picture various things that could be wrong—slow, weak beating? Malfunctioning valves? Restricted blood flow in the arteries around the heart?"

I was careful not to say any of it in a way that might lead or guide her to any specific problem.

"You can also use your hands, to help you detect any malfunction," I reminded her.

In just a matter of seconds she had it—she correctly identified what the problem was.

"You can use this as a point of reference in the future," I said. "Go over what you detected, review what you did and how you detected this information."

When the psychic was ready to proceed, I asked the orientologist if there were any other problems to correct. Now that we knew the psychic was working on the correct subject, she could correct all of the problems whether she detected them or not.

Working Cases on Your Own

If there is no one available to help you, then you can be your own orientologist. Have someone write down the information for you, or download cases from the SilvaHealthCases.com website.

Once you are at your clairvoyant level, open your eyes long enough to read the name, age, location, and gender of the case subject, then close your eyes, relax, and work the case.

After you finish your psychic investigation, open your eyes long enough to read the health information, then close your eyes again and correct the problems.

You can also make a recording based on the Directives for Orientologists below and play it back when you are at your level, to guide you through a caseworking session.

Remember to work only real cases—not fictitious or hypothetical cases. If you work an old case, set your Time Mechanism Device back to the day before the case was submitted.

We do not know of any psychics who are always accurate, every time, so evaluate your proficiency on a sample of 10 cases.

When you are first learning, it is best to work cases on people who have physical problems rather than a mental health disorder.

Also, keep in mind that projecting healing energy to people also energizes you. You are like a pipeline delivering healing energy from higher intelligence to the case subject, and some of it stays with you. That is one of the reasons we feel better after working health cases than we felt when we started.

Special Instructions

1. We do not diagnose; we do not heal. Only medical people have a license to diagnose and heal. We conduct psychic investigation for detection and correction of abnormalities at a distance.

2. We do not perform a psychic investigation of a person when that person is present. For that you need our holistic faith healing course.

3. We do not give our own name to be worked as a case while we are present.

4. We avoid involvement that blocks our ability to function.

5. We do not create problems. We solve problems.

6. Avoid talking about negative things when a person is at deep levels.

7. When you work a case on somebody you know, you never tell them what you think is wrong with them; you never ask them if they have a specific problem; your "suggestion" could influence them, especially if they are highly suggestible.

8. Work with human life before working on animal life, plant life, and the inanimate. Never neglect human life. It is recommended that you work on your family every night just before going to sleep. Correct any problems you detect but don't mention it to them. If the problem never materializes, then assume that you did your job and corrected it before it had a chance to develop physically.

Directives for Orientologists

Here is a script you can use when presenting cases to your partner. You can also make a recording based on this script that you can play to guide you through a caseworking session.

ENTER LEVEL ONE

Enter your center with the 3 to 1 method.

If you have worked cases before, review a case that you were accurate on before working a new one. Let me know when you are ready. (When ready, continue.) I will now count from 10 to 1 to allow your mind to adjust to the specific level where you are going to be accurate and correct on the problem case that I am going to present to you. 10—9—8—7—6—5—4—3—2—1. Your mind has now adjusted to the specific level where you are going to be accurate and correct on the case I am going to present to you.

PRESENT THE CASE

At the count of 3, the image of the body of (give name, age, address, and sex of subject) will be on your screen.

1—2—3 (snap fingers). The image of the body of (give name, age, address, and sex of subject) is on your screen. Sense it, (pause) feel it, (pause) visualize it, (pause) know it is there, (pause) take it for granted it is there.

Slowly scan the body with your sensing faculties, starting at the scalp and moving your sensing faculties downwards inch by inch until you reach the feet. Let me know when you move your sensing faculties from one point to the other. You must keep talking as you go.

As you continue to scan the body with your sensing faculties, continue to talk as you go, and tell me everything that enters your mind about the subject. Whenever you feel that there is a problem, let me know.

(Orientologist: When you notice the psychic getting near the problem area, mentally project a thought or mental picture of the problem. This helps the psychic to develop a feeling for clairvoyance.)

This is a practice session; at this time, let your experience come forth. Accuracy comes with practice. You may feel as though you are making it up, so tell me everything that enters your mind.

(Orientologist: As soon as the psychic detects a problem, have the psychic zoom in on it):

Amplify the selected area or part of the body, zoom in on it, analyze it, and tell me what you detect with your sensing faculties.

When you locate the area of the body that is doubtful, think of the possible problems that could affect this part of the body. Remember: once you detect a problem, apply the corrective measures that you feel are appropriate.

(Orientologist: When the psychic has finished with that part of the body, instruct them to continue scanning the rest of the body.)

After you have corrected what you detected, continue scanning the body, moving your sensing faculties downward inch by inch until you reach the feet.

Keep talking as you investigate; tell me everything that you are inclined to say. You may feel as though you are making it up; this is the correct feeling. Tell me your impressions regardless of whether you think they are right or wrong.

(Orientologist: Be sure to have information written down ahead of time. When you notice the psychic getting near the problem area, mentally project a thought or a mental picture of the problem to the psychic. This helps the psychic to develop a feeling for clairvoyance.

(In the beginning, encourage "hits" by telling the psychic to tell all. Do not say right or wrong until a complete report has been given.

(After a complete report has been given by the psychic, then at that time evaluate the information, tell the psychic what you know about the case, and point out to the psychic the hits so that they can be reviewed by the psychic while at level. During this evaluation, on misses, tell the psychic, "I do not have this information; it could be so."

(On hits, remind the psychic to review the information perceived with the subjective senses, and especially the feeling experienced when the psychic said what they said, in order to establish points of reference while still at level.

(If everything is a total miss, the psychic could have the wrong person; the best thing to do is to present a new case.

(If the psychic also wants to report information on a relationship or business problem, let them do so. If you have information about the situation, then give the psychic feedback on it.

(Be sure to have the psychic send correction for the problems detected, at the completion of a case and before working another case or coming out of level.

(After this is done, you can give the psychic another case by going back to Present the Case above.

(The following is to be said aloud to the psychic when the psychic has completed the caseworking session and is ready to come out of level):

Every time you enter this dimension with the sincere desire to help humanity, you will be helping yourself; your talents will increase and you will become more accurate every time. And this is so.

Thank you. You may come out, 1 to 3, in perfect health.

Discuss the case briefly.

Special Instructions

We do not diagnose. Only medical people have a license to diag-nose and heal. We conduct psychic investigation for detection and correction of abnormalities at a psychic level at a distance.

We do not perform a psychic investigation of a person when that person is present.

We do not give our own name to be worked as a case while we are present.

We avoid involvement that blocks our ability to function.

We do not create problems. We solve problems.

Avoid talking about negative things when a person is at deep levels.

Work with human life before working on animal life, plant life, and the inanimate. Never neglect human life.

It is recommended that you work on your family every night just before going to sleep, because we can often detect problems mentally before they appear in the physical dimension.

If you detect something, do not tell the person about it. "Mind guides brain and brain guides body" so we don't want people thinking about problems they don't have. Just correct whatever you detect, and if it never shows up physically, then assume you were successful in stopping it before it got started.

Part 4
Silva Success Stories

CHAPTER 22

Psychic Senses Solve Many Problems

What is it like to actually use your mind regularly to find solutions to a wide variety of difficult problems?

Amar Ramsinghani, from Nashik, India, has been doing that since he first took the Silva ESP training 30 years ago. He applies what he learned to help people resolve challenges in real estate, health, and more. He also helps animals in distress.

Amar has a long list of successes and was kind enough to share some of them.

Turn Liabilities into Assets and Everybody Wins

"In early 2021, a close friend of mine faced the prospect of financial collapse," Amar said. "His residential project had unsold ready apartments, zero cash flow, and was on the verge of being classified as a Non-Performing Asset (NPA).

"One of the biggest barriers to sales was the location. It stood next to a cluster of hutments, an encampment of huts where many low-income people lived.

"Instead of ignoring this issue, I incorporated it honestly into my subjective communication sessions. I mentally pictured buyers recognizing that reliable domestic help would always be available nearby.

"This shift in perception made sales conversations easier, and what was once a cause of insecurity actually turned into a point of comfort and convenience. The hutments became a feature that made their daily lives easier.

"Best of all, everybody benefited. It was a striking reminder of how ESP, when paired with honesty and clean intention, can reframe weaknesses into strengths.

Many Health Problems Resolved

Amar Ramsinghani has used the Silva mental projection techniques to help many people who were experiencing health problems.

"A young mother named Rashmi, in her seventh month of pregnancy, seemed drained both physically and emotionally," Amar said. "Her gynecologist had diagnosed a dangerously thin amniotic sac ("baby's water bag") and prescribed heavy medication. The situation was critical.

"At the alpha level I pictured the amniotic sac becoming normal and of the right thickness, healthy, stable, and strong, and I consciously invited guidance from higher intelligence.

"Within two days, Rashmi and her husband were intuitively guided to a new lady gynecologist who specialized in natural treatments and immediately discontinued all heavy allopathic medications.

"A follow-up sonography one week later revealed a completely normal and healthy amniotic sac."

More Health Problems Corrected

Amar reported on several other health cases that were corrected soon after working the cases and using mental projection to imagine perfect health. Here are some examples.

Mental projection produced measurable relief in a senior citizen diagnosed with a brain tumor, removing the immediate need for surgery and hospitalization.

A long-suffering father experienced near-instant reduction in vertigo symptoms after targeted programming.

A new mother with a partial stroke regained speech and left-side movement quickly after healing sessions, a dramatic recovery that uplifted the family and ensured proper care for the newborn twin infants.

Animal ESP Helps in Many Ways

The same techniques that help humans can help animals too.

"Focused animal communication helped me connect two lost leopard cubs with their mother, a rare wildlife reconnection that surprised local rescuers," Amar said.

"Many a times I have imagined superimposing an animal's head over my own as we learn in the human anatomy conditioning cycle in the Silva ESP training," Amar said.

"This primarily has helped me to feel the feelings the animal is going through. I generally have been visualizing golden/white light to calm and soothe the distressed animal and establish a deeper connection with it.

"Two leopard cubs had been accidentally separated from their mother during sugarcane harvesting on the outskirts of

Nashik. Local rescuers, under the coordination of wildlife volunteer Abhijeet and supported by Mrs. Shridevi, a longtime animal welfare advocate, safely recovered the cubs. Despite all efforts, however, the mother did not return.

"Time was running out. The cubs were scheduled to be transferred to Sanjay Gandhi National Park, far from their natural territory. Shridevi, who has long championed wildlife rescue and rehabilitation in Nashik, refused to accept defeat. "Knowing about my experience with Silva's intuitive communication techniques, she reached out—and that became the start of an extraordinary collaboration between human intention and nature's intelligence.

"First I entered my level and established a strong golden light band connecting the cubs' hearts to the mother's heart.

"Twice a day I entered the alpha level to connect intuitively with the mother leopard, focusing on calm visualization of the mother leopard reuniting safely with her cubs. Using mental projection and visualization, I pictured her in her natural setting, calm, alert, and longing to find her cubs.

"During these sessions, I used mental projection to sense the mother's emotional state and physical surroundings, requesting her guidance on how best to help.

"Meanwhile, Abhijeet and his rescue team coordinated with the Forest Department, and Shridevi maintained overall communication and moral support from her network in Nashik, ensuring that the team's compassion and focus remained unwavering.

"I felt that the mother leopard was conveying to me that she would return to the spot where her cubs were found the following evening.

"The rescue team waited until midnight, but she didn't appear.

"The next morning, the mother leopard expressed sadness and anger, saying she had come but was disturbed by human activity and passing vehicles. I doubted my senses until I informed Shridevi, who immediately cross-checked with Mr. Abhijeet.

"His confirmation stunned everyone—he said every detail was 100 percent accurate. The area had indeed been crowded with noisy jeeps and villagers that night.

"Upon re-engaging with the mother, I asked the mother for a better solution. I received a vivid image of a clearing about 500 meters away from the road, and said 9 p.m. would be the right time.

"Following her lead, the team set up the cubs at the new location by 8 p.m. At 9:30 p.m. the mother leopard appeared, cautiously approached, and gently carried both cubs into the forest—a perfect reunion witnessed in silence and awe."

More Animal ESP Cases

Here are some more Animal ESP examples from Amar:

In another case, a distraught owner was reunited with her long-lost dog within hours of targeted programming and intuitive scanning, ending her day of anxiety.

Through precise subjective communication and investigation cues, several rare parrots stolen from an animal lover were located and reunited with their owner.

Animal activists partnered with intuitive detection to find a severely abused pet. The animal was rescued and liberated from ongoing harm.

Squillo, an adopted stray dog, was suffering from severe epileptic fits, averaging one every day and a half. After several weeks of mental programming to correct the problem, the seizures were reduced to one every 12 days.

CHAPTER 23

Awakening Your Natural Psychic Gifts

Robert Meyer has always had some psychic ability.

"From an early age I was reading everything I could find at the local library on ESP and ghosts," he said. "I could have read about an ESP technique but have no idea about where I read it or exactly what it might have been."

He tried an experiment in the summer of 1977 to see if he had some ESP that might help him solve a problem, like finding his way if he was lost.

"Navigating to the person's house was something I just wanted to try," he said. "This was a friend so there was some emotional attachment.

"I knew where the person lived, in a town thirty miles away or so, but had no idea of the town's layout.

"I started in the general direction and as I neared the town I stopped at several intersections and literally relaxed a bit waiting for a 'hunch' to decide which way to go.

"I would look in the possible directions and sense the 'gut feeling' for direction. I did know the address, but had no map or other reference to find the street.

"As I reached the neighborhood and saw the street sign, I knew I was there. The house was back in a subdivision and had a reputation of being hard to find."

A few years ago Rob enrolled in a couple of our home-study courses and had another impressive experience.

"I was doing the short relaxation meditation at bedtime, and just as I started to relax, a vision of a young friend popped into mind," he said. "The picture I saw was the type that one might see in a high school yearbook. In this vision my friend spoke but the picture remained still. He said, present tense, 'I'm in a car accident.' As it was late, I didn't have a means of contacting him. The next day I found out he was fine, so I took a breath of relief.

"The next time I saw him, I told him what had happened. He laughed and discounted the whole thing.

"About six weeks later he was in an accident. He fell asleep whilst driving home from work on a Friday afternoon. (He was working two jobs then.) He was virtually uninjured but had fallen asleep, crossed the highway, and hit a fence. Had there been oncoming traffic it might have been very bad.

"I did not try to picture him directly as being okay. I realize now I could have done that; I probably should have known by then. There was a great sense of relief in that I would be able to warn him ahead of time, once I found out the accident had not occurred in real time. One thing I noted in the vision was that he looked fine in the 'image' I saw. I interpreted this to mean he would be okay."

Perhaps Rob's assumption that his friend would be okay was sufficient to alter the course of events that transpired six weeks later.

CHAPTER 24

Using ESP Is Good Business

The right tools and the correct attitude helped a businesswoman through some difficult situations.

Marie-Laure Marrel of Talloires in the French Alps, learned the UltraMind ESP System during the summer of 2023. "I started by reading and applying every exercise during the entire four weeks of José Silva's book *Getting Help from the Other Side*." The book uses the same alternate system for finding your level that we include in the Appendix of this book.

She wrote and asked us a question: "Times have been pretty tough since the covid lockdown. So my question is: How should I set my mind to be worthy of help from higher intelligence, as I am the only one involved in my business, and I do not yet have employees who will also benefit?"

We replied: "I am sure that when you are less distracted by financial challenges, you will do an even better job of caring for your clients. In other words, they will benefit right along with you. As José Silva said, the world was not made for just one person."

She was excited when she replied:

"Actually yesterday I used the Time Mechanism Device for the first time, to figure out at level when the cause of those money challenges occurred in my life and I found between 2015 and 2016.

"So I did a quick search on my computer for the date 2015, and I was amazed as appeared on the screen a verdict of the highest court in France with a judgment in my favor for a legal issue I'd had.

"Do you think it may be linked to the fact that I may still resent that person and what happened that cost me more in cash (and energy) than I was to receive?"

Here is how we replied:

"Nobody can hurt you mentally from a distance. It takes physical force to hurt, and the mind isn't physical. What someone can do is trick you into thinking bad thoughts, and since mind guides brain and brain guides body, if you harbor bad thoughts in your consciousness, you are doing it to yourself.

"I'd go level, use your Time Mechanism Device to go back to the time of the incident, review the problem—the bad thing that happened—then erase it, imagine the good thing that should have happened, move the Time Mechanism Device back to the present and imagine the good things that are going to happen.

"From then on, whenever you think of the incident or the person, immediately dismiss that thought and think about the good work you are doing, the people you are helping, and, as José Silva used to say: Keep in mind what your needs are plus a little bit more."

Concentrate on Solutions

She replied with one more question: "For now, what techniques would you highly recommend, complimentary to your suggestion to dismiss negatives thoughts, to attract new clients?"

We replied: "Remember that we need to concentrate on solutions, not on problems.

"Getting new clients is not the solution. Getting new clients is the problem.

"The solution is serving new clients and helping them get what they want and need."

She had built a strong foundation for success by helping people with health problems.

"I've worked 27 cases, plus one horse that had liver and lung issues and that after treatment won the jumping championship on the weekend!

"My mum had leg pain because of old age and too much walking on holidays, and the day after I worked her case she told me that she spent an entire afternoon dancing!

"Do you recommend I do caseworking on them as much as needed until results show up? Or is it good to do caseworking at a space repeated time?

"Also, when caseworking if I got an image of the person or animal, I went straight to the point, but if not, I found that closing my eyes is not so efficient. I tend to feel sleepy, so I tried something else. Being in a dark room but having my eyes open and defocused seems the best."

Here is the advice we gave her:

"Regarding how much to work on a problem, Mr. Silva said to do as much as you feel you need to do. Sometimes we need to allow a little time for the programming to take effect.

"Always let your feedback guide you. If you are working on somebody once a day and nothing happens, try something different: You could work on them more and see if anything happens, or work on them less and maybe that will produce results.

"If the results are in the right direction—they get better—keep on going, keep doing it, and maybe do even more.

"If the subject gets worse, that's great feedback too. Try something different. We had one case of a young man here in Laredo who had a kidney transplant. He was calling me every morning with an update. There was one area that wasn't improving, so we programmed more. After a couple of days he called and said, 'Program less.' So we didn't work on him that day. The next day he improved and a few days later he was healthy enough to go home.

"The last time I saw him was about 10 years later at the local Holiday Inn. He had gotten married, had a new job—life was wonderful—and he said it was all because of the Silva Method. He was certain he wouldn't be alive if not for the Silva Method and the local Silva graduates who worked on him mentally."

CHAPTER 25

ESP Helps Her Know What to Do and Say

With a few days of practice you can become proficient at using both physical and mental techniques together to solve problems. Begin by completing the Magic 50 Health Cases the way we explained in the final segment of the UltraMind ESP System, Chapter 21.

Jenny Moutou of Queensland, Australia, first took the Silva Method in 1999–2000. "I was expecting my first child and was already highly intuitive," she said, "but I didn't understand the gift it was.

"After completing the course, I kept practicing the techniques and by chance one day found myself on the phone with a colleague. He was home with his child and not in a good way. She was not behaving and his patience had worn thin.

"While I was on the phone with him I got a sense that all was not well. Through the conversation I managed to calm him to a level he could function and be present for his child. After the call I went into a meditative state and continued to work with him. It was only later that I found out he was in such a state he may have taken his own life.

"It was a powerful lesson for how we can dramatically impact people's lives beyond the need for words, and in life changing or saving ways.

"I was relieved to have been of service in this way."

CHAPTER 26

How to Find Lost Objects

Here is a series of emails we exchanged with Grace Ho, a Silva graduate and an occupational therapist who serves on the University of Southern California Board of Councilors. She is also a best-selling author and motivational speaker in Japan.

"With your guidance and the Silva techniques," she wrote, "I feel better than I expected during the first holiday season without my father. Thank you.

"Now I need your help to locate a missing item. I cannot remember where I put my mother's necklace when my father passed away. It should be somewhere in my house, but it isn't where I thought I last put it."

We replied: "Now is when all the Health Caseworking you have been doing to help people can pay off for you and help you find your mother's necklace.

"The first thing I would do, of course, is enter the alpha level, do some deepening, review the most recent, most successful case (or cases), in order to help you be just as successful on this case.

"At the alpha level—your 'center'—at 10 cycles per second, the center of the normal brain frequency spectrum, your mind can retrieve information wherever it is impressed on your brain.

"Go back and recall the last time you saw the necklace. Recall what you were thinking, what you were doing, what did you do next, were there any distractions, and anything else that comes to you."

Adding Some Extra Help

"Another technique that works well is dowsing.

"Objects—like the necklace—absorb and store energy of the person who had it in their possession. So you can walk through the house, anywhere the necklace might be, and desire to sense when you are close to it.

"If you are holding dowsing rods or a pendulum when you do this, they will act as a 'biofeedback' device to alert you when you are close to the necklace. Here is how that works:

"Your mind will detect the energy radiating from the necklace when it is within range of the physical part of your aura, approximately eight meters (25 feet). Since 'mind guides brain and brain guides body' this will cause a reaction in your brain, and since you expect the dowsing rods or the pendulum to move when this happens, they will.

"If the necklace is farther away then you need another technique. That's where caseworking comes in. There is no time or space in the subjective dimension, so you can enter your clairvoyant level the way you learned in the UltraMind ESP training and follow the same procedure as you do when you work health cases.

"Review your most recent case when you were 100 percent successful and this will help you be just as successful again.

"If that doesn't produce the necklace, then you can ask higher intelligence for help. You do that with the MentalVideo.

"Let me know when you find it, and how you found it. It will make a great case study for our next book. A whole lot of people could benefit from hearing how you succeeded in finding the necklace, and how important it is to you."

"I Found It!"

Three days later she wrote: "I found it!

"Thank you so much for your encouragement and support.

"Yesterday, I was at my friend's home when I read your email, celebrating his father's 90th birthday.

"I didn't have self-confidence in terms of using my ESP, because I just started a few months ago. I thought 'Oh, no, I don't have that talent yet.'

"So, today, I am doing New Year's tidying and home decluttering. I saw a wire hanger, ready to throw away, and I remember you said a wire hanger would do.

"My dowsing rod made of the wire hanger looked awkward, and it was moving. (Please see the attached picture at the end of this email.)

"I said to myself, 'See, it is a bad rod. I need to order a good official dowsing rod from Amazon.'

"Then, the second thought came, 'I will throw this dowsing rod anyway, let's try for fun.'

"Holding the rods in front of me, I walked to a small bedroom to fold my laundry. The rod was moving. Again, I said to myself, 'See, the wire of the wire hanger is bent and not straight.'

"So, I went back to folding laundry.

"Then an idea came: 'Wait a minute, I better check the armor furniture.'

"When I opened it, voila! It was there!

"I couldn't believe it.

"I didn't even do the Centering Exercise before the dowsing. I had just finished my lunch and was getting sleepy. I was going to take a nap after the laundry."

Evidently she was close enough to the alpha level to get the job done.

Here is the photo she sent of her homemade dowsing rods:

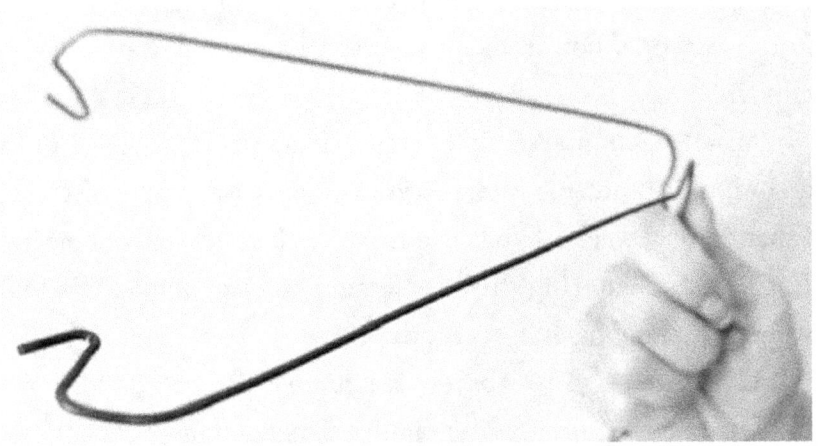

CHAPTER 27

Many Ways an Influencer Uses ESP

Everybody knows to "Stop, look, and listen" before driving into a busy intersection. Reverend Bert Mayne of Schoharie, New York, uses one more sensing faculty to help him stay safe. He explains:

"There is an intersection I travel through often. I live out in a rural area, and this intersection is a necessary part of travel I make every week or so. I use my ESP to check for oncoming traffic before entering the intersection and turning left, as I do when returning from my errands.

"The intersection is barely safe under the best conditions, but by projecting my sensing faculties ahead of me, I get a mental picture of the traffic approaching the intersection. I don't take any more time than necessary to get through that intersection, but with the help of ESP I am always able to make that turn with greater confidence that it's safe to do so."

How to Work a Case on Yourself

Here is how Bert worked a case on himself to find the cause of a problem the doctors couldn't locate.

"A hip operation turned problematic when my femur broke as the struggle to get its vice-grip-like attachment in the socket loosened. As a result my hospital stay suddenly stretched from 'a day or two' to just over two weeks. This was followed by a few months of physical therapy. I started to feel increasing pain along the outline of the metal plate that was used to hold the femur for healing.

"I went to level and detected nothing unusual about the plate, and in my routine post-op visit to the surgeon an x-ray showed nothing wrong with the plate. The surgeon offered no ideas as to what might be causing the pain, other than to suggest more PT.

"When I did another ESP examination of my leg, I found myself directed toward something that ran along the side of the plate and seemed to have some sort of pressure relationship with the plate, as if it were pushing on it at times.

"There was a knot, that I had figured was tense muscle due to the pain, that was so large when the pain was worst that it was visible on the leg surface down by the knee. At level I did a time regression with my Time Mechanism Device to see what its relationship was to the pain.

"I was surprised to find that it was subtle, but noticeable in its preceding of the pain by a short time. I had thought it was likely a result of tension caused by the pain, and not a possible cause, or part of a cause. But it now seemed the other way around.

"My next visit to the orthopedic folks was with a physician's assistant. Interestingly, after a brief bit of being puzzled about the increasing pain, she said it sounded like it just might be a tightening of the IT band. That was a thing I'd never heard of, but it matched my impressions of something that ran along the edge of the metal plate. I got an instant sense that she was onto the root cause.

"I was given exercises to stretch the Iliotibial Band, and am feeling less and less pain as the days go by. So, what MRI, x-ray, and surgical knowledge and skill couldn't figure out, a skilled PA and Effective Sensory Projection solved."

Using ESP to Motivate People

How do you persuade people to come to church?

You announce a great topic that everybody wants to know more about.

How do you keep their attention once they get there?

You talk to them on their level without talking down to them.

If you are a talented singer-songwriter like Reverend Bert Mayne, you use the Silva techniques to expand your consciousness to include all of humanity as well as higher intelligence.

"I'm still preaching at two churches," Reverend Mayne said. "I start way ahead of time, going to level and using ESP to see if there are any specific things I need to include in the sermon to be sure it benefits the greatest number of people, and to see if there are any specific things that some individual really needs to hear.

"Projecting my sensing faculties out to look for a topic provides ideas for sermon content, and also on how to pique curiosity, and it always comes through."

Once he has a topic and ideas on how to present it, he enters the alpha level and uses another technique. "I sometimes create a 'brain trust' for sermon writing," he explains.

"I always used to help my 'Time for Children' talks by creating a little old lady, sort of the quintessential grandmother, who was also the greatest Sunday school teacher ever.

"She used to help me come up with all sorts of images, and examples that kids could grasp to get my point across. It never resulted in that kind of talking down to the children you sometimes hear, which was good because I always believed you should get the same point across in the children's sermon and in the adult sermon."

Part 5
Advanced Strategies and Techniques

CHAPTER 28

How to Improve Your ESP

by José Silva

Once you have completed our ESP training you can learn to function at the alpha level with your eyes open, so that you can use your ESP to help you solve problems and make better decisions at any time.

You can learn to function at the alpha level with your eyes open, so that you can use your ESP to help you solve problems and make better decisions at any time.

During the day, your brain dips into the alpha level about 30 times per minute. But the time in alpha is very short, only microseconds. In all, your brain may be in alpha five seconds out of every minute.

With practice, you learn to stay at alpha for longer periods of time. You can simply evoke the feeling of being at your level and you will have alpha functioning. You must avoid focusing your eyes, but maintain "defocused vision," the way you do when you are "daydreaming."

When you are talking with someone, you can simply desire to attune to that person, and use the so-called "daydream mechanism" to function as a psychic.

How to Get to Your Clairvoyant Level Instantly

Here are the specific instructions to help you learn to develop alpha functioning full-time so you can get to your clairvoyant level instantly when you need it:

Work the first 50 cases as soon as possible.

You worked the first 10 cases during the final session of the UltraMind ESP System by using the standard 3 to 1, 10 to 1 method to enter your clairvoyant level. Evaluate your accuracy over that group of 10 cases.

If you are satisfied with your results on the first 10, then shorten the ritual for entering level by using the 10 to 1 method to enter your level, and work 10 more cases. Just count from 10 to 1 to get to your clairvoyant level.

You are becoming conditioned now, so you don't want to add to the ritual. Do less and less of the ritual until you don't need it anymore.

Evaluate your progress after you work those 10 cases, and if you are satisfied, then reduce the ritual again and enter your clairvoyant level with just the 3 to 1 method.

Evaluate those 10, and if you are satisfied with your results, enter your clairvoyant level by closing your eyes and taking a deep breath, and as you exhale, enter your clairvoyant level.

Evaluate those 10, and if satisfied, practice working cases with your eyes open and defocused, like when you are day-dreaming.

Using ESP with Your Eyes Open

After you have worked the Magic 50 Health Cases successfully, all you need to do is daydream about your clairvoyant level, and you will be there.

Remember: Do not attempt to "focus" your eyes on anything. Maintain "defocused vision." You will be perceiving directly with your mind—with visualization and imagination—and indirectly with your eyes.

Just stare in the direction, and then you work as though you're at your level without even taking a breath. Just take it for granted you're there. You will be just as accurate.

You are reducing the ritual for entering your level because you don't need it anymore. You're going to function as naturally as you function right now.

The only difference, anybody looking at you would see your pupils dilate, then contracting when you come out level. If they're looking at your pupils, they know when you're in and when you're out. That's the only way they can tell.

You can speak like I'm speaking now, and still be at your level because you're not trying to see anything. People say the pupils of my eyes were dilated. That's the alpha level.

Desire It and It Is There for You

Once you have learned to function this way, your desire will activate your psychic senses. It is just like having a desire to hear or not to hear; you're either there or you're over here listening to this song. You can direct your attention. You can be here, you can be there. You decide what you need and automatically you're there.

Now, where there's a need to do something like to see, you have to be at the visual perspective. If you want to hear, you have the audio range perspective and so on. It depends on what you desire.

Desire Is a Tuning Mechanism

Your desire is your tuning mechanism, but you must know what you desire. You must have previously established the points of reference in order to want that again, which means to desire it.

If you do not establish a point of reference, you don't know what you want, you don't know where to go. You don't even know that it exists; how can you desire that? How do you tune to it?

We get to these dimensions and establish points of reference at the inanimate matter kingdom so that you can desire it later, to be tuned to that frequency or dimension or whatever it is that's there. The same thing happens to the plant or vegetable kingdom, animal kingdom, human life kingdom, and this is how you evolve.

CHAPTER 29

Increase Your Desire and Motivation

One of the most valuable things that can help you when you need to solve a problem or reach a goal is faith.

"Mind guides brain and brain guides body" so doubts will lead you in the wrong direction, while faith will increase your chance of success.

José Silva's formula for faith has three components:

Desire belief, and expectancy, which is also known as hope.

Desire

The more important something is, the more motivation you will have to get it. So the first thing you can do to increase your faith is to go to your level and think of all of the benefits of solving the problem or reaching your goal. The more reasons you have, the stronger your motivation.

The more motivated you are to do this, the faster you will learn, and the more effective you will be.

So let's take a moment to do some motivation.

The Motivation that Really Matters

There are some talented motivational speakers who can evoke a lot of emotion and use that emotion to motivate you. That can be quite powerful, but it wears off over time.

You already have something even more powerful that you can use to motivate yourself from within: your mind.

You just need to know how to use it for motivation, and then you can motivate yourself in just a few minutes, any time you need it.

The way to motivate yourself, to increase your desire, your enthusiasm, and your energy level, is:

Think of the benefits that come from the work you are doing.

Let's do that right now:

Begin by thinking of benefits that you will receive when you improve your ability to take care of your financial needs.

How many reasons can you think of?

It will reduce the stress in your life. Improve your credit score. You will be able to buy more of the things you want, and do more of the things you want to do. You will be able to help your family and loved ones more.

The more reasons you think of, the stronger your desire will be.

Now to increase your desire even more, let's think of who else will benefit when you learn and apply and use these new skills:

Your family will benefit. How will members of your family benefit? Think of each family member, and how they will benefit.

If you have children, they will no longer be limited in their opportunities to participate in activities with their peers. When they are asked to donate to a worthy cause, they can donate as much as their friends donate. They can have clothes just as nice as their friends, and attend events with their friends. This will help them to develop social skills and increase their self-esteem and self-confidence.

Your spouse or significant other will benefit. So will your parents, your siblings.

Who else will benefit when you use these new skills to help you take care of your financial needs?

How about businesses that you do business with? The owners, their employees, all of them will benefit when you are able to pay them on time and do more business with them.

Do you get the idea?

You can think about these things at the alpha level, at your center, and you will come up with even more ideas, and you will think of even more people who will benefit from your success

Then enter your level with the 3 to 1 Method (Chapter 12), start thinking again, and you will come up with more reasons.

If you have twice as many reasons, you will have twice as much desire.

How Motivation Helped José Silva Succeed

José Silva began his research because he wanted to help his children make better grades in school so they would do better in life. That is very important for many parents.

José Silva went beyond that. When neighbors noticed what he was doing, they asked him if he would also help their children. He did, and never asked for anything in return. When he saw how appreciative they were for his help, he had even more desire to help.

Health and healing became a big part of his research. He never turned down a request to help, and he never accepted any kind of compensation, not even reimbursement for travel expenses.

More and more people were benefiting from his work, and as they did, more new discoveries about the mind and human potential were revealed to him.

Belief

Belief comes from experience—from successful experiences.

We may think that we can do something but we never know for sure until we actually do it. And that's what builds belief: successful experiences.

The more successful experiences you have, the stronger your belief. This is a powerful component in the formula for faith.

We may "think" we can do something, but we don't really *know* until we actually do it.

That is one of the reasons why it is so valuable to practice working health cases. It reassures you of two things:

1. You are helping people who need help.
2. The more you practice, the less self-destructive doubt you have.

As you continue to practice projecting your mind and mentally correcting health problems, you may find yourself developing a profound sense of the common bond we all share with one another.

Expectancy, Also Known as Hope

The third component is simple: Keep the solution in mind.

Whenever you think of the project, immediately visualize the solution image that you created previously. Do not dwell on the problem, or the current situation. Change that image to an image of the solution, the desired end result.

Take it for granted that your project has been completed in the subjective (mental) dimension and will soon materialize in the physical dimension.

The Most Important Formula in the Course

There is a formula in the course that sums up all of this. It is the last paragraph before you come out of level. Mr. Silva wanted it to be the last thing you hear at level before you go to sleep and go through at least one sleep and dream cycle. That gives your brain an opportunity to "install" the program and file the information where it needs to be.

When we observed that "This is a statement of unselfishness isn't it?" he replied:

"If it weren't for that attitude, we wouldn't have the Silva Method today."

Here is the formula:

"You will continue to strive to take part in constructive and creative activities to make this a better world to live in, so that when we move on, we shall have left behind a better world for those who follow. You will consider the whole of humanity, depending on their ages, as fathers or mothers, brothers or sisters, sons or daughters. You are a superior human being; you have greater understanding, compassion, and patience with others."

CHAPTER 30

Improve Your Caseworking Accuracy

There are several excellent techniques in the Directives for Orientologists in Chapter 21 to help you become an outstanding psychic.

The most important thing in the beginning is to get experience. Experience is more important than accuracy. That's why the orientologist tells the psychic:

"Continue to talk as you go, and tell me everything that enters your mind about the subject. Whenever you feel that there is a problem, let me know."

It is just as important to be wrong sometimes as it is to be right.

If your information is never incorrect, you will not be able to learn the difference. So . . . say everything that comes to mind, realizing that not all of the information you are giving will be correct; this is necessary in order for you to learn.

That's why the orientologist tells the psychic:

"Continue to talk as you go, and tell me everything that enters your mind about the subject. Whenever you feel that there is a problem, let me know."

It is not about "guessing" the name of the illness, or drawing conclusions about what you detect.

As the Directives say, accuracy comes with practice.

Examples of How We Learn

One new psychic who was working cases for the first time announced that the subject's left lung was diseased. He could tell because it was so much darker than the right lung.

After he had finished his investigation, I told him that the subject's left lung was healthy. "Does that mean the right lung has been removed?" he asked. "That is correct." He had detected the information accurately.

Another time there was a man taking the course with us in the Bahamas who had done a lot of meditating. He had great visualization, very clear images. He followed instructions and gave a detailed account of what all of the organs and blood vessels and nerves and bones and muscles of his subject looked like. He didn't detect any obvious problems.

But I noticed something as he described his journey through the case subject's body: He said that the subject's spleen seemed to glow, and light was shining onto another part of the body, and he mentioned light a couple more times.

So when he finished I told him that he had mentioned light several times, and suggested he go back and check those areas more closely. Every one was a problem area, and he was able to discover exactly what kind of problem it was: illness, something broken or damaged, etc.

We are sharing these experiences to show you that when you are learning nobody is grading you on how accurate your information is. The most important thing in the beginning is to get as much experience as you can.

Correlation Method

Prerequisite: Magic 50 Health Cases (Chapter 21)

Nobody is right every time. Even the best psychics average about 80 percent overall accuracy. With practice, a good Silva psychic can often sense when they are not detecting information but are just "making it up."

But suppose you have a situation where you need accurate information. That's when you can use the Correlation Method.

Here is José Silva explaining a situation like that when a troubled wife didn't know if her husband was dead or alive.

The Missing Pilot Case
by José Silva

This is a very beautiful case. A woman came to us, to our group of graduates in Perryton, Texas, and she had a problem. She said she wanted to see whether our trained clairvoyants could give her some information on what was troubling her.

Her problem was that so many months before, her husband, a US Air Force pilot, had been shot down over Vietnam, and she had not heard from him. She wanted to know, "Can you people tell me if he's dead or alive?"

That's a beautiful project. Why not.

What we did was take 10 trained clairvoyants and separated them in teams of two, then told them, "Go home. Here's the information, the name of the individual, his age, approximate relation, so forth. Tell us about this individual, what you can tell us."

They came back the next day, each one with a report. We had five teams of two, with five reports. We correlated the information:

Where two or more said the same thing, we made one report. Where only one said something, we eliminated it.

Now, the consensus of the correlated information was saying that the man was alive, that he was flying very low and barely had time to use a parachute, but he was alive. He had hurt himself because he'd been flying very low. He had hurt his back and his right leg, but he was alive.

The woman kept thinking about it. She said, "I should have asked another question."

I said, "What is it?"

"When would I know that your people are right?"

You see, we could have been wrong, and if so, she might be waiting all of her life for him to come back and never come back.

That's another good project, so let's do it again. Let's go find out when she will know that we are correct.

Here we go. The same teams were back home again. During the night, they did this. The next day, they came back with the five reports. We correlated the five reports. This was in March. The consensus was that she would know that we were right by the first part of July. March to July is a long time. I wish it had been the next month. It was a long time for her to be waiting. What was going to happen was going to happen.

On the 3rd of July, an announcement came out from Hanoi that they were deliberating on freeing some prisoners. No names were mentioned.

On the 19th of July, the announcement came out that they had freed three prisoners. There were three pilots, and one was this woman's husband.

When he came home, she told him what had happened. He called all our group who worked on his case, and he agreed and approved and confirmed everything they said:

- Flying very low
- Could barely use a parachute
- Had hurt his back and his right leg

This man, he was a major then, took the Silva Mind Control course immediately and became a graduate.

CHAPTER 31

Let Your Hands Help Your Mind

Prerequisite: Silva ESP training (Chapters 12–21)

Your mind can help your body, and your body can help your mind.

If you want to improve your visualization and imagination, use your hands. Do what babies do: They see something for the first time and they reach out to touch it. It helps them reinforce what they see.

My best friend in college was blind, and through him I met most of the other blind students. When first meeting them they would often ask if they could feel my face, so they would know what I looked like. Blind people taking the Silva training often have excellent visualization, and are excellent psychics.

Use Your Mental Magnifier

When you are working a health case, or working on any other kind of problem, you can fine-tune your sensing ability by simply snapping your fingers.

As we impressed during the study of metals conditioning cycle in Chapter 16, whenever you need to increase the illumination or amount or size of anything, just snap the fingers of your right hand slightly, and expect the change to take place. For a decrease, or to return anything back to its original state, snap the fingers of your left hand slightly, and expect the change to take place.

If you are communicating mentally with a family member or friend or associate, you can use your finger-snapping controls to help you hear them more clearly. Or you can turn the volume down.

Use Your Hands to Detect Problems

There are other ways your subjective sense of touch can help you. When working health cases, I get a lot of information through my hands.

When I first scan the whole body, I reach out and imagine the subject's body is between my two hands, and I move my hands up and down rapidly, about two seconds to go the length of the body.

Sometimes my hands stop, and I investigate that part of the body.

Sometimes my hands move in and out—closer together and farther apart—and this lets me know the person has arthritis.

When I investigate inside the body, if my hands tingle I know there is a problem with the brain or nervous system.

When I hold the heart my hands move slightly, and the amount and speed of the movement lets me know the condition of the heart. The same with the lungs.

After I first started doing this I became curious, so I opened my eyes and took a peek. Sure enough, my hands were actually moving physically.

This can be an excellent way to detect information. When you can feel it, then you know exactly what the subject is experiencing.

Please keep in mind that what you are feeling is not your problem; it is the subject's problem. If the feeling is too intense, then use your finger-snapping controls to reduce it or eliminate it entirely.

Also remember that in order to correct health problems at a distance, we need to use mental images. The images you have of a healthy body will reinforce and strengthen the soul mold, which is a mold of a perfect human body. It is both cohesive and attractive, and attracts matter to conform to the blueprint of perfection. You can read more about this in Chapter 32.

Finger Dowsing

Back around 1991, when our *Sales Power* book had just been published, we went to Memphis, Tennessee, to present a special edition of the Silva course to salespeople. The local Silva lecturer had given us a list of local Silva graduates and prospects to call.

Our sales consultant had been adamant that when we had a list like that we should not try to guess which ones to call but should call everybody on the list. But after calling a couple of dozen people, I began to get restless.

I wondered: Why not use my ESP? if I am 80 percent accurate, then eight out of every 10 people I call will benefit.

So I began looking down the list, and since there were a lot of names on each page, I put my index finger on the page and moved it down the list of names quickly as I looked at them.

Then my finger stopped moving down the list. That surprised me. I hadn't made any conscious decision to stop scanning the list.

So I dialed that number and the person who answered was very interested in what we were doing and said they would attend.

When I went back to scanning the list, it happened again . . . and again . . . and again . . . Every time my finger stopped and I called the number, I found somebody who was interested in the course. My finger was acting like a dowsing rod and locating what I was looking for.

We haven't conducted any formal research on this, but other Silva graduates have talked about doing the same thing, so as long as it continues to work, we'll continue to use it.

Let us know when you find new ways to apply these techniques and we'll share with others. You can contact us through our website.

CHAPTER 32

Health and Healing Techniques

If you have a health problem, the first thing to do is to use the technique in the Silva Centering Exercise:

"If you have a health problem, practice for 15 minutes three times a day."

José Silva said that the 10 cycles per second alpha brainwave frequency, the center of the brain's normal frequency range, reinforces your body's natural functions from the center.

A magnetic field pulsing 10 times per second stimulates subatomic particles. Many users have reported excellent results in correcting health problems when they hold a pulsing magnetic field directly over the afflicted area, about a quarter of an inch (about 6 cm) away from it.

The US National Institutes of Health website has several reports of various scientific studies confirming that this works. One report, about using a low-frequency pulsing electromagnetic fields on patients with knee joint osteoarthritis, concluded:

"According to the results of this study it can be concluded that LFPEMF is a very effective therapeutic procedure in treatment of patients with knee joint osteoarthritis." The article is in the nih.gov website. www.ncbi.nlm.nih.gov/pubmed/23654012

All you need is an audio recording of the Alpha Sound, a tapping sound that taps 10 times per second, and an audio player with a speaker that uses a permanent magnet along with an electromagnet to produce sound. That will produce a pulsing magnetic field.

You can get an Alpha Sound recording from our website.

Better Tasting Food That Is Better for You

You can use mental projection to help you select the best food at the supermarket. You could establish points of reference first by studying your favorite foods at your level the way you did in the Projection to Home exercise (Chapter 15).

When preparing and serving food, you can imagine projecting thoughts of good health into the food. Perhaps that explains the origin of the custom of taking a moment to bless your food before eating it.

Programmed Water

In Chapter 5 we discussed how a scientist named Bernard Grad used "programmed water" to help plants grow faster.

You can program water to help accelerate healing.

To program the Special Glass of Water Technique, you can enter your level with the 3 to 1 Method, do a 10 to 1 deepening countdown, and then program the following script to "install" it in your brain. Then follow the instructions and do what it says.

(Impress this information while you are at your level):

Impression of information for your benefit, programming the Special Glass of Water Technique to Serve as Medication, for yourself or for someone else.

Get a water glass and fill it with water. While holding the glass of water, find a comfortable sitting position, close your eyes, and enter your level with the 3 to 1 method.

Hold the glass of water with your fingertips. Your fingers should not be touching each other, but should be spread up and down the height of the glass of water. The fingertips of your left hand will be close to the fingertips of your right hand, but will not be touching the fingertips of your right hand. The thumb of your left hand will be on the opposite side of the glass from your fingertips; it will be close to your right thumb, but will not be touching it.

Program the water to correct a health problem by using the 3-Scenes Technique. In the first scene, directly in front of you, visualize the subject with the health problem. In the second scene, approximately 15 degrees to the left of the first scene, mentally picture the person drinking the water and imagine the person drinking the water, and the problem being corrected as a result. In the third scene, which is 15 degrees to the left of the second scene, imagine the person in perfect health.

A Worldwide Healing Hotline

Prerequisite: Know how to work health cases

Silva graduates sometimes desire help through a "healing hot line" so that their programming efforts will be reinforced by the programming of other graduates.

The Alpha Uni-Mold is just such a "hot line" technique.

It is a technique that you can use at any time, on your own, and you can be certain that other graduates will reinforce your programming.

While you can use the Alpha Uni-Mold at any time, there is a specific time that you can apply it and know that other graduates are programming at the same time.

When to Program

To make it simple, many members of the Silva International Graduate Association (SIGA) enter their level (10 cycles alpha) at 10 o'clock at night local time and use the Alpha Uni-Mold.

Marcelino Alcala, a longtime Silva instructor and director in Puerto Rico and the Caribbean in the 1980s, is the one who came up with the idea of 10 cycles alpha at 10 p.m.

If Silva graduates all around the globe do this, then any hour of the day or night you can tap into this powerful spiritual healing network and get help for yourself and your loved ones who are ill or injured and need physical healing.

The Alpha Uni-Mold concept uses the principle of the soul mold, and elements of the concept of communicating with higher intelligence at the center of the galaxy.

How It Works

To use the Alpha Uni-Mold to correct any health problem that needs correcting, enter the alpha level and visualize a mold on your Mental Screen.

This mold is like the entrance to a tunnel. It looks like a silhouette in the shape of a perfect adult human body. This mold is deep enough so that we can place in it all of the people who need help.

Imagine each subject you desire to help backing into the Alpha Uni-Mold. Imagine each person to be just the right size to fit into the mold.

To help all of the subjects in the Alpha Uni-Mold, those placed there by others as well as those placed there by you, imagine a beam of white light, tinged with blue, coming from the center of your forehead into the mold.

You can imagine that this healing light comes to you from the center of the galaxy and flows through you as you direct it to different parts of the mold.

Use this beam of bluish-white light to energize the mold from head to feet.

Energize the brain, the right and left hemispheres, all of the brain. Project this healing energy to the entire head area.

Imagine the energy going all the way through the mold, energizing the brains and heads of everybody in the mold.

Move on down the body, energizing the entire body: All of the organs in the chest area: the heart, lungs, thymus gland. Energize the stomach, the intestinal tract; the pancreas, liver, gall bladder, kidneys.

Energize the entire skeletal system, the entire nervous system, the entire circulatory system.

When you have done this, then be sure to imagine each subject in perfect health.

While you are projecting in this manner, keep in mind that this is correcting the cause of the problem.

CHAPTER 33

ESP for Better Relationships

Psychometry and mental projection are excellent ways to improve both family and business relationships.

If information about a person is stored in an object they carried with them, imagine how much more powerful it will be when you use the 3-Scenes Technique to impress a "program" into an object.

You can go into your child's bedroom and place the palms of your hands on one of the walls and use the 3-Scenes Technique (Chapter 15) to program the bedroom. You can imagine energy being transmitted from the palm of your right hand and then looping around and being collected by the palm of your left hand.

You can program "lucky charms" too. Athletes have been doing that for years: They have a special pair of socks they were wearing when they won a big event and now they wear those same socks every time they compete. Some people think it is just superstition. We see the science behind it.

You can also program your workplace to help create the kind of workplace that will be most beneficial to you, your associates, your customers, and the overall business.

Add Mental Rehearsal to Your Toolkit

Prerequisite: Silva ESP training (Chapters 12–21)

Whether it is communicating with your children or parents or spouse or business associates or angry neighbors or ... well, you get the idea:

Whatever your task, first practice it mentally, at the alpha level.

This is ideal for selling, buying, negotiating, interviewing for a job, parenting, athletic competition, and more.

It also works for solo activities, like writing a book. That's correct: I do it in my mind first, then I go to the keyboard and often something better appears on the screen.

When you use a technique like this to build rapport and interact with people on a deeper level, they will sense whether you sincerely want to do what's best for everybody concerned or if you just want whatever is best for you.

To make sure we have the right attitude as indicated in the Laws of Programming (Chapter 8), we have found it valuable to work a couple of health cases before doing this kind of programming.

You can enter your level and impress this technique at the alpha level so that it will be ready when you need it.

Mental Rehearsal Formula

First enter your level and do some deepening, then when you are ready program yourself like this:

Impression of new information, programming a formula-type technique: the Mental Rehearsal technique.

When you need to take action to solve a problem and you desire to rehearse mentally ahead of time, enter level 1 with the 3 to 1 method and then project yourself mentally to the place where you will perform the problem-solving activity.

Once you have projected yourself mentally to the place where you will perform the activity, study the environment the way you studied your living room.

Remind yourself that you want to do what is best for everybody concerned, then imagine yourself doing what you need to do. Imagine yourself improving and progressing toward a successful conclusion.

Notice how you feel as you are performing the activity. Imagine how you feel as you begin the activity the way that you desire. Imagine how you feel as you progress in the activity. Imagine the feeling of success and the sense of accomplishment as you succeed in materializing your solution.

A Technique for Enhanced Intuition When You Need It

Prerequisite: Silva ESP training (Chapters 12–21)

There are many "healers" in the Laredo area, on the Texas–Mexican border. Here is a technique that uses something José Silva learned in his research of holistic faith healers.

One of the things observed is that they channel healing energy through their own body and use this extra energy to help solve problems. It helps both the person who needs healing and also the healer.

Why do holistic faith healers gain energy when doing this? It is like oil flowing through a pipeline: Some of the oil sticks to the inside of the pipes.

Now if there were only a way to recirculate some of that energy, to keep it flowing so that more of it "sticks."

Fortunately there is. You can capture the energy that flows out of your fingertips, recirculate that energy, and reuse it.

There are many uses for this, including enhanced ESP. Simply bringing together the very tips of your first two fingers and thumb of either hand causes your mind to adjust to a deeper level of awareness for enhanced ESP.

It is helpful when you need to recall someone's name or the key point you need to convey in your presentation, or you need to determine what the other person wants to get from their interaction with you or selecting food that is good for you or any other beneficial purpose.

Here is the formula the way we impress it at level. Just enter your level with the 3 to 1 Method and when you are ready "install" the program in your bio-computer brain.

Please note: You need to touch the tips of your thumb and the first two fingers so that they form a circle. Not the flat part of your fingers where your "fingerprints" are. Energy comes out of the end of your fingers, so touch the tips.

You can enter your level and impress this technique at the alpha level so it will be ready when you need it.

The Formula

We will now impress information for your benefit, programming a formula-type technique, the Three Fingers Technique for Enhanced Intuition. At this time, bring together the tips of the first two fingers and thumb of either hand. (pause)

By bringing together the tips of the first two fingers and thumb of either hand, your mind adjusts to a deeper level of awareness for enhanced intuition.

Enhanced intuition results in better communication, enabling you to solve more problems.

More Strategies and Techniques

Other techniques you can benefit from include these two from Chapter 20:

- Time Travel, using your Time Mechanism Device.
- Superimposing the subject's head over your own to learn what they are thinking and what their real wants and needs are.

CHAPTER 34

Programming for Financial Success

Prerequisite: Silva UltraMind ESP System

Would you like to know how José Silva programmed to get the money when he needed it?

Once you learn our system you can program the same way he did so you can meet your financial needs.

The wrong way to do it is to program to get more money.

"Getting more money" is the problem.

Remember: "Mind guides brain, and brain guides body."

"We move in the direction of our dominant thoughts."

You don't want your dominant thoughts to be about your need for money, because that is the problem and you don't want to reinforce the problem.

Why Do People Give Us Money?

We all care about our own needs. Nobody is inclined to give you money just because you ask them for it.

An author named Bob Berg, who wrote a book about being a Go-Giver, says that nobody is going to buy from you because you have a quota to meet, or because you're a nice person who really means well.

No company is going to hire you simply because you need a job, or are a nice person who promises to work hard.

They will buy from you, or they will hire you, because they believe that *they* will be better off by doing so than by not doing so.

This means that the best way for you to get what you need is to concentrate on how you can bring value to the other person, or to the company that you want to do business with.

Wouldn't it make sense that the most valuable communication skill that you can learn is to find out what the other person's wants and needs are, and to figure out how you can do more than anyone else to give them what they want and need?

When you do this, people begin to feel good about you. They like you, they will trust you, and they will feel safe and comfortable with you. They will want to do business with you.

How José Silva Programmed for Money

José Silva said, "It is easy to get a million dollars if you need it. First give 10 million dollars' worth of service to humanity, and if you need a million dollars you will get it.

"Not because you *want* it," he added, "but because you *need* it."

He said that whenever he needed more money he went to his level and thought about ways he could provide a new product or service that people would benefit from, and "I kept in mind what my needs were . . . plus a little bit more."

In addition to doing some creative thinking at the alpha level, you can also use the MentalVideo Technique that we covered in Chapters 7 and 15 to ask higher intelligence for guidance to help you make the best choice.

"When you need money," he told Silva instructors during an Instructor training session in 1995, "always remember whatever your needs are.

"You only get help from the other side when your intentions are that whatever you are doing is to help improve conditions on the planet for more than yourself, not just yourself.

"You may want business, and business with others, which means that you must have planned already what the money will be used for.

"Money is not just to be had; it is to be put to work.

"So always consider the benefits that are derived for more than just you. If it is only for you, and you don't care about any-body else . . . big question mark.

"And whenever you ask, remember: Ask for no more than what you need, but *do* ask for *no less* than what you need. That's good enough.

"What you need means: What plans do you have? If they are big plans, you need big something. If they are little plans, you need little something.

"So what your needs will be depends on how big your plans are. That's what your needs will be."

You can enter your level and impress this technique at the alpha level so you will be ready when you need it.

How to Program for Money When You Need It

When you need money, program in the following manner:

Program for the service that you intend to give. Enter the alpha level and think about how you can provide new or better products or services. Think about people who are not currently benefiting from your products or services and how you can locate them and communicate the value of your products or services to them.

Once you have identified opportunities, then program yourself to follow up and take action to provide more products or services. As you do this, keep in mind what your needs are, plus a little bit more.

When you help people in the area they need, or to help them better, and you need more money in order to do that, the money will come.

When you have bills to pay or you need to order supplies, purchase new equipment, pay off a debt, instead of programming to get the money, program to take care of what you need it for. Program for the end result, not just the money.

Get other people involved who will also benefit from your success. Bring more people around you who will benefit from your programming. It will provide more energy for your project.

Alpha Decision-Making

Prerequisite: Silva UltraMind ESP System

We make many decisions every day involving our family, our career, our health, and personal and spiritual growth and more.

José Silva has a simple technique to help us make the difficult decisions. It is a valuable tool you can add to your decision-making toolbox.

You can enter your level and impress this technique at the alpha level so you will be ready when you need it.

Elimination Technique for Decision-Making

When you need to analyze an important project and make decisions about it, here is how to proceed:

When there are two options and you desire to know which is better, you bring both to mind: Option Number 1 and Option Number 2.

Then clear your mind from thinking about the project by thinking of something else that is not relevant to the project at all, such as: I need to buy a new pair of shoes tomorrow.

Then immediately start thinking again about the two options. The one that enters your mind first is usually the right one, and the one you should go for.

When there are more than two options, work two at a time using the same procedure. The one that comes to mind first can be compared to a third option.

Always retain the option that enters your mind first, until you have dismissed all except one option.

That option is the best one.

Help from Expert Consultants

Prerequisite: Silva UltraMind ESP System

You can use your ESP to access all of the wisdom of the past and present when you need to solve a problem that will improve living conditions. Here is one way to obtain the specific information you need.

You can enter your level and impress this technique at the alpha level so you will be ready when you need it.

Expert Consultants Formula

We will now impress information for your benefit, programming the Expert Consultants Technique.

To use the Expert Consultants Technique, enter your clairvoyant level with the 3 to 1, 10 to 1 method.

At that time, you can create a duplicate of an individual you respect in the area of expertise you need.

You may create a duplicate of your leading competitor, or a top attorney, a high-priced market consultant, a government expert, a religious leader, even a historical figure. Visualize that expert and mentally ask for advice regarding the special problem you are working on.

You do this by directing your question mentally to the expert, then clear your mind for a moment by thinking of a different subject. When you begin to think of the problem again, an answer comes.

It may feel as if you are making it up. It may feel as if you are putting words in the expert's mouth, as if it is your answer, not the expert's. That is the correct feeling. Accept it.

Be sure to thank your consultant before coming out of your level.

How to Create Instant Rapport

Prerequisite: Silva UltraMind ESP System

You can create rapport with someone you have never met or spoken to by using mental projection at the alpha level before you meet with them. Then when you meet them in person, they will have a good feeling about you, as though they have known you for a while and know they can trust you.

Here is the technique. You can enter your level and impress it at the alpha level so it will be ready when you need it.

Instant Rapport Technique

Programming a formula-type technique: Instant Rapport

When you desire to pre-program yourself to have instant rapport with a prospect, client, or customer, proceed as follows:

When you are in bed and ready to go to sleep, enter your level and program yourself to wake up automatically at the best time to program to establish rapport with the person. Then go to sleep as usual.

The first time you wake up during the night or in the morning, sit up in bed, and enter your level with the 3 to 1 Method.

Once you are at your level, bring together the tips of the thumb and first two fingers of either hand, or both hands. Think about your client and the meeting you are going to have with the client. Tell yourself mentally, "Whenever I bring together the tips of the first two fingers and thumb of either hand, as I am doing now, my client will sense that I am there to help them, and they will know that they can trust me."

Use Reverse Psychometry to Infuse Objects with Information

In Chapter 19 you learned how to extract information about people from objects. You can reverse the process to infuse objects with information by programming business cards and gifts to be subtle reminders of your goodwill, personality, and integrity.

To do this, hold the item between your hands, enter your level, and use the 3-Scenes Technique to illustrate how your products or services will be beneficial to your clients.

You can carry programmed business cards with you and they will continue to absorb information about you. Be sure you follow the Laws of Programming, and let your personality and the real you shine.

Appendix

APPENDIX A

A Glimpse into the Future

José Silva wrote the following in *I Have a Hunch: The Autobiography of José Silva.*

In business, there will be far more executives who will be able to use clairvoyance to make accurate business decisions by determining the needs of the public ahead of time. Executives will be healthier, and thus more valuable to their companies, because they will use their clairvoyant level to maintain their own good health by relieving stress and relaxing.

Government leaders of all nations will project into the future mentally to detect the needs of their people and be prepared when those needs arise. Government leaders, using their clairvoyance, can sense whether the people they are dealing with are sincere, and also sense what future plans others have. At this time, wars between nations will cease, because the element of surprise will be nil.

Law enforcement agencies will use their mental abilities to help them capture criminals and virtually put crime to an end. On the other side of the issue, people with criminal tendencies will be identified and taught to function in a superior manner that makes it unnecessary to engage in criminal activity to achieve what they desire.

There will be an abundance of natural resources in the world of tomorrow, because petroleum engineers and geologists will use clairvoyance to dowse for minerals—without using a divining rod. They will learn to detect oil and other minerals underground, the depth, quantity, and quality, and will reduce the number of misses or dry holes. Archaeologists, meteorologists, metallurgists, and others will use clairvoyance in their specialties to gather more information that will help them improve the quality of their work.

Astronomers will find they can use their clairvoyant mind to explore the universe much more economically than by launching spacecraft. The same can be said for the human who at some time or other must travel from one inhabited planet to another, and who leaves the body behind and acquires a new body more suited for that environment. The clairvoyant astronomer may also find other civilizations that reside at other dimensions on this and other planets and satellites, civilizations that cannot be detected with our limited objective senses, because these civilizations can exist at other channeled frequencies that require a different set of sensing faculties.

Industrialists will be able to use clairvoyance to better determine what to manufacture for future consumption. Stock-market specialists and investors can use clairvoyance to mentally project into the future and sense the future needs of the population so as to make the correct choice of stocks that will have the greatest demand. Financiers can use clairvoyance to make the best decisions on what projects to invest in. Through their clairvoyance, they can determine which potential projects will provide the greatest service to humanity and thus help make this world a better place to live while earning enough money for their own needs in the process.

Pilots and operators of all types of vehicles will use clairvoyance to free themselves from accidents. When people function at their clairvoyant level, not only do they strengthen their immune system, but they also strengthen their intuitive factor, which is a function of the right brain hemisphere. A person with a very strong intuitive factor will subconsciously move, function, or act in a timely way to escape dangers. Consequently, I say people who are not clairvoyant have no business operating vehicles, endangering their own lives and the lives of others.

Ranchers and farmers, who are responsible for providing the food for human survival, will use clairvoyance to select proper breeds and proper seeds to use. In other words, they will be better able to select the best of everything used in the production of food for the human race on this planet.

A clairvoyant rancher who breeds very expensive breeds of cattle and uses the artificial insemination system can use his clairvoyance to prepare the animal for a higher percentage of takes, reducing the percentage of losses, and resulting in a more economical venture.

To be most successful, the rancher must always keep in mind that the primary purpose of being a rancher is to supply the survival needs for as many human creatures of the Creator as is possible. The means to carry out such an intention will be supplied from higher up and will be according to the sincerity of your intentions.

Farmers who plant the seeds, care for the crops, and collect the harvest to supply the demand for food to maintain life in the creatures of the Creator can, above all, use their clairvoyance to produce more and better quality crops.

From their clairvoyant level, farmers can select the proper tract of land, prepare the land properly, plant the seeds timely, and while doing so influence the seeds to be fertile and productive at the maximum.

The Vital Role of Parenting

Parents are the only ones really responsible for the continuation of the existence of the human race on this planet. They serve as doorways through which humans enter this planet. Parents should be the newcomers' fundamental teachers, models, and guides.

We call the newcomers our sons and daughters, but they are not ours; they don't belong to us. They are only placed in our charge. We have been selected to play the role of consultants and guides for them, and to care for them and supply all their needs. It is going to cost us just as much to care for them as it cost our parents to care for us. This is how we pay the system back for what we cost our parents.

All humans arriving on this planet have been sent by the same power for the same purpose by the same means, and regardless of what we have called race, creed, or color, the whole world is their home.

We who have come before them took it upon ourselves to define and establish borders so that newcomers to the planet may or may not cross those borders.

Keep in mind that newcomers to this planet are traveling on their own path in the universe and arrive on this planet individually. After their short stay, they leave this planet individually and again continue traveling on their own path in the universe. Nobody belongs to anybody. We all belong to our Creator, and we are here to help our Creator in the molding of creation.

The titles of fathers and mothers are given to the ones who are to take care of the newcomers to the planet, and to care for them until they are capable of caring for themselves. The fatherly and motherly love that we manifest to the newcomers to this planet is a program established within us by our Creator to abide by our obligation to take care of them.

Why are we to play the roles of teachers, models, and guides? Simply because we got here first and should know our way around and should also know what direction we should guide them. It is our obligation to guide them correctly in the direction they should take; this is the responsibility we have toward our Creator.

All parents need to be, and should be, clairvoyants. We need to use these intuitive and prophetic abilities to properly guide the newcomers of this planet. It is our obligation toward our Creator, remember? We have a tendency to forget it.

My recommendation for humans who desire to be parents is, first, to be trained in clairvoyance so you will have a better chance to be correct on the selection of the person who is to be your lifetime partner. Non-clairvoyants are only 20 percent accurate when selecting. No wonder there are so many divorces. On the other hand, the clairvoyant who has practiced clairvoyance can be 80 percent accurate or better. Of course, this helps in selecting the correct lifetime partner. People who practice living together before marriage manifest the nonuse of either brain hemisphere; some keep on changing partners until perhaps they find the right one. Some animals have better systems than this.

The child's best teacher and programmer is always the child's mother. The female, by nature, is always more spiritual and more intuitive. Clairvoyant parents can help their clairvoyant sons and daughters, through the use of clairvoyance, to correct bad habits and establish good ones. They also teach them to develop their own control, so that nobody will ever control them and put them to work as slaves selling candy, flowers, and books in airports and on street corners.

A very important message for parents is to remember that whoever gets into your child's brain and mind first is the winner. So, parents, be sure that you, to be the winners, get into the minds and brains of your sons and daughters first through the use of clairvoyance. This will make the child the real winner.

A New Phase of Human Evolution

We are the pioneers of this new phase of human evolution, we four billion plus, who are developing the new science of psychorientology on this planet, the science of tomorrow—today. Our immediate goal is to bring these research findings to as many people as possible in the shortest possible time.

Now I have shared with you my discoveries. It is time for you to make your own discoveries, as you practice and learn to use your clairvoyant abilities. As we say to people who have never done it, "The greatest discovery you will ever make is the discovery of the potential of your own mind."

APPENDIX B

Save the Planet Project

José Silva made the script of the Silva Centering Exercise available under a "Creative Commons Attribution-Non-Commercial-No-Derivatives License" for non-commercial use, so feel free to copy it and use it to guide family, friends, and associates to level.

If you want to use it commercially please contact us.

Here are his guidelines on how to read the Centering Exercise to someone.

How to Read the Silva Centering Exercise
by José Silva

The Silva Centering Exercise helps people discover an inner dimension, a dimension that they can use to become healthier, luckier, and more successful in achieving their goals.

When a person learns to function from this inner dimension, the person automatically becomes more spiritual, more human, healthier, safer from accidents, and a more successful problem-solver.

In order for a person to use this inner dimension, the person needs to hear the Silva Centering Exercise a total of 10 hours, and to follow the simple directions in the mind exercise.

How to Proceed

The Silva Centering Exercise can be read for 10 hours in one day, or read once a day, or once a week.

Take time at the start and at the completion of reading the Silva Centering Exercise. Take a break between each reading of the exercise.

Keep a record of reading time until 10 hours has been accumulated by the listener.

You can read to one or to several persons at the same time.

How to Read

When reading the Silva Centering Exercise, read in a relaxed, natural voice. Be close enough so that the listener can hear you comfortably. Read loud enough to be heard, and read as though you were reading to a seven-year-old child. Speak each word clearly and distinctly.

Have the listener assume a comfortable position. A sitting position is preferred, but the most important thing is to make sure the listener is comfortable. If uncomfortable, the listener will not relax as much and will not get as much benefit from the exercise.

Avoid distractions, such as loud outside noises. There should be enough light so you can read comfortably, but not extremely bright lights. If you wish, you can play the Alpha Sound (available at our website) gently in the background to help the person remain at the 10 cycles per second alpha brainwave level. Do not play music; the frequency of music is constantly changing, and we want the person's brain to beat at a steady 10 cycles per second.

If the person shows any signs of nervousness or appears to be uncomfortable, stop reading and tell them to relax and make themselves comfortable. When they are comfortable and ready, then continue.

Take your time when you read; there is no need to rush.

The complete script of the Centering Exercise is in Chapter 12.

Alternative Way to Find the Alpha Level

(**Note**: It is not necessary to do this if you are learning by listening to a recording of the Centering Exercise or having someone read the Centering Exercise to you as you learned in Chapter 12.)

by José Silva

I will give you a simple way to relax, and you will do better and better at this as you practice.

I will also give you a Beneficial Statement to help you.

This is how you train your mind. You relax, lower your brain frequency to the alpha level, and practice using imagination and visualization.

Because you cannot read this book and relax simultaneously, it is necessary that you read the instructions first, so that you can put the book down, close your eyes, and follow them.

Here they are:

1. Sit comfortably in a chair and close your eyes. Any position that is comfortable is a good position.

2. Take a deep breath, and as you exhale, relax your body.

3. Count backward slowly from 50 to 1.

4. Daydream about some peaceful place you know.

5. Say to yourself mentally, "Every day, in every way, I am getting better, better, and better."

6. Remind yourself mentally that when you open your eyes at the count of 5, you will feel wide awake, better than before. When you reach the count of 3, repeat this, and when you open your eyes, repeat it. ("I am wide awake, feeling better than before").

You already know steps one and two. You do them daily when you get home in the evening. Add a countdown, a peaceful scene, and a Beneficial Statement to help you become better and better, and you are ready for a final count-out.

Read the instructions once more. Then put the book down and do it.

Learning to Function Consciously at the Alpha Level

As stated previously, you learn to enter the alpha level and function there with just one day of training when you attend the Silva UltraMind ESP Systems live training programs. You can use the audio recordings to learn to enter the alpha level within a few days with either a Silva home-study program or the free lessons at the SilvaNow.com website. You can also record the Silva Centering Exercise in Chapter 12 and listen to it, or have someone read it to you.

If you have already learned to enter the alpha level by one of those methods, you can skip the following instructions for practicing countdown deepening exercises for the next 40 days.

If not, then follow these instructions from José Silva:

When you enter sleep, you enter alpha. But you quickly go right through alpha to the deeper levels of theta and delta.

Throughout the night, your brain moves back and forth through alpha, theta, and delta, like the ebb and flow of the tide. These cycles last about 90 minutes.

In the morning, as you exit sleep, you come out through alpha, back into the faster beta frequencies that are associated with the outer conscious levels.

Some authors advise that as you go to sleep at night, you think about your goals. That way, you get a little bit of alpha time for programming. The only trouble is, you have a tendency to fall asleep.

For now, I just want you to practice a simple exercise that will help you learn to enter and stay at the alpha level. Then, in 40 days, you will be ready to begin your programming.

In the meantime, I will give you some additional tasks that you can perform at the beta level that will help you prepare yourself so that you will be able to program more effectively at the alpha level when you are ready at the completion of the 40 days.

Your First Assignment

If you are using the Silva Centering Exercise (also known as the Long Relaxation Exercise) on the SilvaNow.com website to enter the alpha level, then you can skip the information that follows.

If you do not want to use the recording of the Silva Centering Exercise, and you have not attended a Silva seminar or used one of our home-study courses to learn to enter the alpha level, then you will need to follow the instructions here to learn to enter the alpha level on your own.

Here is your alpha exercise:

Practice this exercise in the morning when you first wake up. Since your brain is starting to shift from alpha to beta when you first wake up, you will not have a tendency to fall asleep when you enter alpha.

Here are the steps to take:

1. When you awake tomorrow morning, go to the bathroom if you have to, then go back to bed. Set your alarm clock to ring in 15 minutes, just in case you do fall asleep again.

2. Close your eyes and turn them slightly upward toward your eyebrows (about 20 degrees relative to your face). Research shows that this produces more alpha brain wave activity.

3. Count backward slowly from 100 to 1. Do this silently; that is, do it mentally to yourself. Wait about one second between numbers.

4. When you reach the count of 1, hold a mental picture of yourself as a success. An easy way to do this is to recall the most recent time when you were 100 percent successful. Recall the setting, where you were and what the scene looked like; recall what you did; and recall what you felt like.

5. Repeat mentally, "Every day in every way I am getting better, better, and better."

6. Then say to yourself, "I am going to count from 1 to 5; when I reach the count of 5, I will open my eyes, feeling fine and in perfect health, feeling better than before."

7. Begin to count. When you reach 3, repeat, "When I reach the count of 5, I will open my eyes, feeling fine and in perfect health, feeling better than before, feeling as though I have slept the right amount of revitalizing, refreshing, relaxing, healthy, wonderful sleep."

8. Continue your count to 4 and 5. At the count of 5, open your eyes and tell yourself mentally, "I am wide awake, feeling fine and in perfect health, feeling better than before. And this is so."

These Eight Steps Are Really Only Three

Go over each of these eight steps so that you understand the purpose while at the same time become more familiar with the sequence.

1. The mind cannot relax deeply if the body is not relaxed. It is better to go to the bathroom and permit your body to enjoy full comfort. Also, when you first awake, you may not be fully awake. Going to the bathroom ensures you're fully awake. But in case you are still not awake enough to stay awake, set your alarm clock to ring in 15 minutes so you do not risk being late with your daily schedule. Sit in a comfortable position.

2. Research has shown that when a person turns the eyes up about 20 degrees, it triggers more alpha rhythm in the brain and also causes more right brain activity. Later, when we do our mental picturing, it will be with your eyes turned upward at this angle. Meanwhile, it is a simple way to encourage alpha brain wave activity. You

might want to think of the way you look up at the screen in a movie theater, a comfortable upward angle.

3. Counting backward is relaxing. Counting forward is activating. 1–2–3 is like "get ready, get set, go!" 3–2–1 is pacifying. You are going nowhere except deeper within yourself.

4. Imagining yourself the way you want to be—while relaxed—creates the picture. Failures who relax and imagine themselves making mistakes and losing frequently create a mental picture that brings about failure. You will do the opposite. Your mental picture is one of success, and it will create what you desire: success.

5. Words repeated mentally—while relaxed—create the concepts they stand for. Pictures and words program the mind to make it so.

6–8. These last three steps are simply counting to 5 to end your session. Counting upward activates you, but it's still good to give yourself "orders" to become activated at the count of 5. Do this before you begin to count; do it again along the way; and again as you open your eyes.

Once you wake up tomorrow morning and prepare yourself for this exercise, it all works down to three steps:

1. Count backward from 100 to 1.

2. Imagine yourself successful.

3. Count yourself out 1 to 5, reminding yourself that you are wide awake, feeling fine, and in perfect health.

40 Days That Can Change Your Life for the Better

You know what to do tomorrow morning, but what about after that? Here is your training program:

- Count backward from 100 to 1 for 10 mornings.
- Count backward from 50 to 1 for 10 mornings.
- Count backward from 25 to 1 for 10 mornings.
- Count backward from 10 to 1 for 10 mornings.

After these 40 mornings of countdown relaxation practice, count backward only from 5 to 1 and begin to use your alpha level.

People have a tendency to be impatient, to want to move faster. Please resist this temptation and follow the instructions as written.

You must develop and acquire the ability to function consciously at alpha before the mental techniques will work properly for you. You must master the fundamentals first. We've been researching this field since 1944, longer than anyone else, and the techniques we have developed have helped millions of people worldwide to enjoy greater success and happiness, so please follow these simple instructions.

Silva Resources

The only authentic José Silva courses that have not been changed or altered by someone else after his passing:

SilvaMethodUltraMind.com

Free Introductory Lessons: SilvaNow.com

Health cases to work and to submit: SilvaHealthCases.com

Official José Silva Website: JoseSilva.net

Home Study Courses and Workshops

Discount code: **ESPMC** at SilvaMethodUltraMind.com.

Holistic Faith Healing, Choose Success, UltraMind ESP, Sales Power, Business Management, Better Relationships, Claim Your Creative Heritage, Fitness and Sports, Weight Loss

Additional Resources

Cleve Backster's research: *The Secret Life of Your Cells* by Robert Stone

Brice Lipton: www.BruceLipton.com

John Mihalasky: Included in *Silva UltraMind Systems ESP for Business Success* by José Silva Jr.

Wilder Penfield: *The Mystery of the Mind*

Phineas Parkhurst Quimby, *The Quimby Manuscripts*, first published in 1921 by Pantianos Classics, new illustrated edition edited by Horatio W. Dresser and published in 2017

Help Your Friends and Loved Ones

If you found this book useful and would like for other people to benefit from it, please consider leaving an honest review with the bookseller. Thank you.

More Books by These Authors

Creative Coincidences: The Next Phase of Human Evolution, by José Silva and Ed Bernd Jr.

In *Creative Coincidences* José Silva reveals how to use your mind to influence the coincidences in your life. "A coincidence," he told us, "is God's way of helping without showing His hand."

Includes step-by-step instructions, case studies, real-world examples, and answers to frequently asked questions.

eBook and Audio editions published by G&D Media; hardcover, paperback, and large print published by Silva Books.

For more books and to follow these authors:

amazon.com/author/josesilva

amazon.com/author/edberndjr

Also by These Authors:

José Silva's Everyday ESP: A New Way of Living

Silva UltraMind Systems ESP for Business Success

Silva UltraMind Systems Persuasive Thoughts: Have More Confidence, Charisma, & Influence

Free Your Magnificent Mind

Expand Your Magnificent Mind

José Silva's Choose Success Master Course

Sales Power, the Silva Mind Method for Sales Professionals

Jose Silva's Guide to Mental Training for Fitness and Sports

Jose Silva's Guide to Effective Decision Making and Goal Setting

www.ingramcontent.com/pod-product-compliance
Lightning Source LLC
Chambersburg PA
CBHW071706120626
46550CB00001B/130